A. PAUL MAHAFFY

PRIVATE COMPANY SHAREHOLDER GUIDE

CARSWELL®

ISBN 978-0-7798-2215-7

A cataloguing record for this publication is available from Library and Archives Canada.

Composition: Computer Composition of Canada Inc.

THOMSON REUTERS

CARSWELL, A DIVISION OF THOMSON REUTERS CANADA LIMITED

One Corporate Plaza
2075 Kennedy Road
Toronto, Ontario
M1T 3V4

Customer Relations
Toronto 1-416-609-3800
Elsewhere in Canada/U.S. 1-800-387-5164
Fax: 1-416-298-5082
www.carswell.com
E-mail www.carswell.com/email

For Cynthia, again

Acknowledgments

In the fall of 2008, I began to notice that part of my business law practice was changing. Instead of clients asking me for help in buying and selling shares in private companies, they were asking me for help in determining their rights as shareholders in an effort to resolve some problem they had. My practice seemed to be more advisory than transactional, tending more to dispute resolution than closing deals.

As the credit crunch of 2008 became the great recession of 2009, many of my clients realized that they were stuck with their private company shareholdings. There would be no initial public offering or sale to a strategic buyer for a while to provide them with an exit from their investment. And there would be no additional financing for their company from outside sources which might allow the company to grow and cause their own shareholdings to appreciate in value.

But even though they were resigned to the fact that they would remain shareholders for some time, they were not prepared to remain as passive, as uninvolved, as unquestioning, towards the company as they had been before. They wanted, in other words, to become active shareholders. They wanted to know what they were entitled to as shareholders of a private company, sometimes for no other reason than to avoid being taken for granted.

I then realized that my clients could use a guidebook that set out all of their rights as private company shareholders to meet their desire to be better informed, regardless of any further desire they might have to enforce their rights if the circumstances warranted enforcement.

Although most of them were experienced investors in publicly listed companies, many held shares in just one private company; often their employer or a company owned by their relatives or close friends. Many had never asked the company about their rights as shareholders for fear their inquiries might be perceived as untrusting or insulting.

This book is intended to facilitate shareholder self-help, and I'm grateful to my clients for sharing their experiences and concerns and giving me the insight and awareness needed to write it.

I'm also very grateful to Sarah Payne and Todd Pinsky of Carswell whose patience and encouragement made completing this book possible.

Contents

Dedication iii
Acknowledgments v
Introduction 1

WHAT IS A PRIVATE COMPANY? 3
WHO IS A SHAREHOLDER? 4
BASIC SHAREHOLDER RIGHTS AND EXPECTATIONS 4

Individual Statutory Shareholder Rights 7
CORPORATE RECORDS 8
Right to Copies of Certain Corporate Records 8
Right to Examine Shareholder List 9
Right to Receive Shareholder List 9
DISSENT AND APPRAISAL 9
FINANCIAL STATEMENTS 10
Right to Receive Financial Statements 10
RECEIPT OF COMPANY DIVIDENDS 10
RECEIPT OF COMPANY PROPERTY ON DISSOLUTION 11
SHARE CERTIFICATES 12
Right to Receive Replacement Share Certificate 13
SHAREHOLDER MEETINGS 13
Right to Requisition Meeting 13
Right to Solicit Proxies 14
Right to Submit Proposals 14
Right to Vote 15

Collective Statutory Shareholder Rights 17
AMALGAMATION 18
AMENDING ARTICLES 20
AUDITORS 21
Right to Remove Auditor 21
BY-LAWS 21
CONTINUANCE 23
DIRECTORS 24
Right to Remove Directors 24
Right to Restrict Directors' Powers 24
LIQUIDATION AND DISSOLUTION 24

SHAREHOLDER SQUEEZE-OUT 25
STATED CAPITAL 26
Right to Increase Stated Capital 26
Right to Reduce Stated Capital 27
TRANSFER OF ALL OF THE ASSETS 27

Additional Shareholder Rights 29
CONVERSION RIGHTS 30
DILUTION PROTECTION RIGHTS 31
DIVIDEND RIGHTS 32
INFORMATION RIGHTS 34
LIQUIDATION RIGHTS 34
NOMINATION RIGHTS 35
PRE-EMPTIVE RIGHTS 36
REDEMPTION RIGHTS 36
REGISTRATION RIGHTS 38
VETO RIGHTS 39
VOTING RIGHTS 39
WITHDRAWAL OR LOSS OF RIGHTS 40

Buy-Sell Rights 41
FIRST REFUSAL RIGHTS 42
PIGGYBACK RIGHTS 44
DRAG-ALONG RIGHTS 45
TRANSFER RIGHTS UPON CERTAIN EVENTS 46
VALUATION OF TRANSFERRED SHARES 47
SHOTGUN RIGHTS 48
AUCTION RIGHTS 49

Unanimous Shareholder Agreements 51
REASONS FOR AN AGREEMENT 53
BOARD AND MANAGEMENT REPRESENTATION 54
MAJOR DECISIONS 56
USE OF PROFITS 57
BANK FINANCING AND GUARANTEES 58
PRE-EMPTIVE RIGHTS 58
MANDATORY SHAREHOLDER FUNDING 59
NEGATIVE COVENANTS 60
Non-disclosure Covenant 61
Non-solicitation Covenant 61
Non-competition Covenant 62
Enforcement of Negative Covenants 63
FAMILY LAW COVENANTS 64
MISCELLANEOUS MATTERS 65

Shareholder Meetings 67
ANNUAL MEETINGS 68
SPECIAL MEETINGS 68
PLACE OF MEETINGS 68
NOTICE OF MEETING 69
ADJOURNMENT OF MEETING 69

PREPARATION FOR A MEETING 70
CONDUCT OF THE MEETING 70

Director Duties 73
FIDUCIARY DUTY 75
Disclosing Conflicts of Interest 76
Avoiding Misuse of Corporate Opportunity 77
DUTY OF CARE 77
Business Judgment Rule 78
OTHER DIRECTOR DUTIES 79
Approval of Financial Statements 79
Appointment of Officers 80
Authorizing Payment of Commissions 80
Borrowing 80
Compliance with CBCA and Company Charter 80
Declaration of Dividends 81
Filling Director and Auditor Vacancies 82
Fixing Remuneration 82
Issuance of Shares 82
Passing By-laws 83
DIRECTOR INDEMNIFICATION AND INSURANCE 83

Governance 85
BENEFITS OF GOOD GOVERNANCE 86
RESISTANCE TO GOOD GOVERNANCE 86
PRESSURES TO IMPLEMENT GOOD GOVERNANCE 87
RECOMMENDED GOVERNANCE STRUCTURES AND PRACTICES 88
The Board and Independent Directors 89
Audit Committee 89
Nominating Committee 90
Compensation Committee 90
Code of Business Conduct and Ethics 90
Director Orientation and Continuing Education 91
Regular Board Assessments 91
IMPLEMENTING GOOD GOVERNANCE 91

Dispute Resolution and Remedies 93
MEDIATION AND ARBITRATION 94
DERIVATIVE ACTION 96
OPPRESSION REMEDY 97
Family Businesses 99
OTHER COURT APPLICATIONS 100
Calling of Meeting 100
Compliance with CBCA 100
Fix Fair Value of Shares 100
Investigation of Company 100
Liquidation and Dissolution of Company 101
Rectification of Records 101
Removal of Auditor 101
Restrain Holding of Meeting 102

Set Aside Contract 102
Settle Controversy over Elections 102

Conclusion 103

Endnotes 109
Introduction 109
Chapter 2 - Individual Statutory Rights 110
Chapter 3 - Collective Statutory Rights 111
Chapter 4 - Additional Shareholder Rights 112
Chapter 5 - Buy-Sell Rights 112
Chapter 6 - Unanimous Shareholder Agreements 112
Chapter 7 - Shareholder Meetings 113
Chapter 8 - Director Duties 113
Chapter 9 - Governance 115
Chapter 10 - Dispute Resolution and Remedies 116
Chapter 11 - Conclusion 117

Index 119

Introduction

Becoming a shareholder of a private company can involve a variety of motivations and expectations. Perhaps there's a desire to help family members or close friends by providing start-up funds for their new business. Maybe there's an opportunity as an employee to become part-owner of an employer and have a say in how it is operated. Or possibly there's a chance to make a lot of money should the company be sold to a strategic buyer or go public.

Whatever the reasons for someone to become a shareholder, the rights a shareholder enjoys may not be considered important at the time, if considered at all. But when the company fails to meet the shareholder's expectations later on, the shareholder's rights then take on much greater significance. What was perceived as a one-time transaction often turns into a more lasting relationship; one that may no longer be very harmonious or easy to escape from.

This relationship often changes, especially when new shareholders arrive on the scene. Growing companies in need of capital continually access additional, possibly institutional, sources of outside money, sources which may impose their own ways of doing business once they arrive. The original shareholders may feel that they have to do what the newcomers tell them to do as part of the sacrifice to be made for accepting new money.

But the changes that occur aren't necessarily bad, just different, and may well be for the better of everyone concerned, including the original shareholders. The changes may lead to good company governance, which may simply be good business.

This book is intended to make the reader a more knowledgeable private company shareholder, better prepared to assert his rights but guided by more realistic expectations when attempting to deal with the changes that may occur.

Not every shareholder wants to know the same things about a private company. Some shareholders just want to know about the company's financial performance, or whether their dividends are likely to remain constant or increase. Others just want to know how to sell their shares when the opportunity arises, or perhaps how to buy more shares if the company continues to prosper. Others may want to know how to get their ideas considered by management, while others may simply want to know what to do when things go badly wrong.

This book will look at what rights a private company shareholder is given by statute and under the common law generally. It will also discuss additional rights a shareholder may acquire by contract, and examine some of the governance practices followed by private companies to provide additional shareholder protection. The impact of shareholder meetings and shareholder agreements on how a shareholder is able to exercise his rights will also be reviewed, as well as the basic duties company directors are expected to perform.

Along with the benefits flowing from these various rights, the shareholder assumes certain burdens. A private company shareholder should be an active participant in the company, not a passive investor, in order to fully derive such benefits. This book will describe some of the obligations which must be fulfilled and actions taken by the shareholder so that his rights and expectations can be realized.

This book, however, is not about buying and selling shares. There are already numerous books available on how to value and transfer private company shares, how to research and conduct due diligence on a company's business, and how to negotiate and document a purchase and sale transaction, including this author's *Business Succession Guide* also published by Carswell.

Although many private companies in Canada are incorporated under provincial companies legislation, this book will generally refer to companies incorporated under the *Canada Business Corporations Act*[1], or CBCA. Because most provincial companies acts are modelled after the CBCA, many of the ideas expressed in this book will apply to shareholders of most private companies, wherever incorporated in Canada. However, the reader should be aware that minor differences do exist and should consult the provincial act that may govern any particular private company.

In order to be gender neutral and in place of he/she, this book will alternate between genders by chapter when referring to a shareholder.

WHAT IS A PRIVATE COMPANY?

Most corporations in Canada are owned by either a single shareholder or a small number of shareholders. They have been traditionally described as private companies, though more recently have been called "closely-held" companies to differentiate them from other companies with many more shareholders but which are not "public" companies. A public company is usually regarded as a company that issues its securities to the public, whereas a private company does not.

A private company is not specifically defined in the CBCA but is often taken to be a company that is not a "distributing corporation", which is defined in the CBCA.[2] It is also often taken to be a company which has "private company restrictions" in its articles of incorporation or other charter documents as prescribed by provincial securities legislation. These restrictions generally limit the number of shareholders, prevent share transfers without, for example, approval by a majority of directors or shareholders, and prohibit solicitations to the public to subscribe for company securities.[3]

For the purposes of this book, the term private company will be used in its traditional context, as a company that does not offer its securities to the public and which has a relatively small number of shareholders (with a maximum of 50). It will not be a distributing corporation within the meaning of the CBCA.

One of the reasons why shareholders of private companies can become confused about their rights and have slightly enhanced expectations of what the company should do for them is the expanded set of rights enjoyed by shareholders of distributing corporations. The CBCA imposes additional requirements upon distributing corporations and provides their shareholders with additional rights. For example, the requirements for an audit committee and shareholder proxy solicitation, or the need to comply with take-over bid rules, which are imposed by the CBCA on distributing corporations, do not apply to private companies.

Even though a private company may seem "private" because much of its financial information is not publicly available, certain corporate information about the company is far from confidential. For example, the names and addresses of its directors and the location of its head office can be found by searching the records of the Corporations Directorate of Industry Canada.[4] A list of its shareholders, indicating their names, addresses, and the number of shares they each hold, can be requested upon payment of a reasonable fee by not just the shareholders but also by the creditors of the company.[5]

WHO IS A SHAREHOLDER?

While the term "shareholder" is not a precise legal term, it is often taken to mean, at least in the private company context, the person who is recorded as the holder of a share on the share register maintained by the issuing company. The share may or may not be evidenced by a tangible share certificate. If it is, the person whose name appears on the face of the certificate is not necessarily the owner, since it may have been endorsed by that person and become a bearer certificate, possibly making the bearer the owner.

For the purposes of this book, as is the case under the CBCA, the person named as a shareholder in a company's share register will be regarded as a shareholder.[6]

Often a person becomes a shareholder by first submitting an offer or subscription to the company, followed by an acceptance or allotment by the company. Subject to any pre-emptive rights (described later in the *Additional Shareholder Rights* and *Unanimous Shareholder Agreements* chapters), the company's directors are empowered under the CBCA to issue shares at such times, to such persons, and for such consideration as they may determine.[7] Since shares are not to be issued until the consideration is fully paid in money, or an equivalent value in property or past services,[8] a person to whom shares are issued without payment is not a shareholder.

A person may also become a shareholder by way of a transfer of previously issued shares from existing shareholders or their legal successors, including by way of transmission from the estate of a deceased shareholder.

BASIC SHAREHOLDER RIGHTS AND EXPECTATIONS

A shareholder usually invests in a private company's shares with the hope of receiving some return on that investment. The return may come as dividends representing a portion of the company's profits, as well as upon the sale of the shares if they are sold for more than their purchase price.

While the shareholders may own the company's equity, they don't play an active role in the day-to-day operations of the company's business. They may elect the directors, consider the company's financial statements and approve certain actions which may fundamentally change the nature of the company or its business, but they have very little say in how the company is operated. That's the role of the board of directors.

But the shareholders generally expect that the board will ensure the company is operated properly in order that their desired return on investment will happen eventually.

And they generally expect that they can't lose more than their investment. After all, one of the main advantages of investing in a company is its "limited liability". Except in a few exceptional circumstances, shareholders are not liable for the debts and other obligations of the company and they put no more at risk than the amount they have paid for their shares.[9] Such circumstances include the improper decrease of capital, or upon the dissolution of the company and distribution of the company's remaining property for a period of two years thereafter, or under a unanimous shareholder agreement. Even though the company may lose money or incur liabilities well in excess of its assets, the shareholders are not required to pay more than they have already invested. Such is not the case when someone invests as a partner in a general partnership.

While these few rights and expectations may appear to many shareholders of private companies to be the only rights and expectations to which they are entitled as shareholders, this book will attempt to illustrate how they are entitled to a lot more. Whether they are prepared to fully pursue all they are entitled to becomes a more complicated question for them to answer. While the *Dispute Resolution and Remedies* chapter sets out how shareholders might seek redress for their grievances, the cost, time and uncertainty of outcome associated with litigation may deter them from acting further.

However, since the shares of private companies are not readily marketable, the option of "walking with their feet" and selling their shares, which may be available to the shareholders of public companies, is seldom available to private company shareholders.

Individual Statutory Shareholder Rights

As a general rule, individual shareholders of a private company all have the same basic statutory rights so long as they are all holders of shares of the same class. If the company has only one class of shares, the holders are equal in all respects and are entitled to vote at shareholder meetings, receive any dividends that are declared, and receive the remaining property of the company upon its dissolution.[1] However, so long as the company is ongoing, shareholders don't have rights to any of the company's underlying assets.

One of the exceptions to this general rule relates to issuance of a series of shares within the same class. The articles of the company may authorize the issuance of one or more series which have different rights, restrictions and conditions from any other series within the same class; provided a series is not given a priority in the payment of dividends or return of capital over any other series of the same class that is outstanding. A series may be created by the directors at their discretion without specific approval by the shareholders if the articles permit the directors to do so.[2]

Another exception relates to the shareholder's contractual rights, ordinarily achieved through a shareholder agreement with the other shareholders, which may restrict or expand upon the shareholder's statutory rights.

The equality of the shareholders can also disappear when more than one class of shares is created by the company. The rights to vote, to dividends and to receive property upon dissolution need not be attached to just one class of shares, and a number of additional rights can apply to one class but not another.[3] These may include redemption rights, preferences to receive dividends or a return of capital, conversion rights, and a number of other rights described in greater detail in the chapter *Additional Shareholder Rights*.

This chapter discusses the various rights shareholders of a private company have, regardless of how many company shares they hold (with exceptions for the right to requisition a meeting or make a proposal, discussed below). They can exercise these rights on their own, without the need to act collectively with any other shareholders in an effort to make something happen. These rights are effectively individual rights, in contrast to the rights discussed in the next chapter which involve shareholders' collective rights which are exercised at a shareholder meeting.

Although some of the individual rights described in this chapter can only be exercised in connection with a shareholder meeting, or by way of a resolution signed by all of the shareholders in lieu of a meeting, they nonetheless represent a shareholder's individual action.

CORPORATE RECORDS

Right to Examine Corporate Records

Shareholders of a private company are entitled to examine certain corporate records during the usual business hours of the company.[4] These records consist of the company's articles of incorporation and by-laws, any unanimous shareholder agreement, all minutes of meetings and resolutions of the shareholders, copies of government filings identifying the company's directors, and the securities register.[5]

However, the shareholders do not have the right to examine the company's accounting records or those records containing the minutes of meetings and resolutions of the directors. One exception to this is the right of a shareholder during usual business hours to examine any disclosures of interest a director or officer may have made to the company, whether such disclosures have been recorded in the minutes of director meetings or in separate documents.[6]

Right to Copies of Certain Corporate Records

The shareholders are entitled, at no charge, to take extracts from those records which they may examine.[7] Each shareholder may also request one copy of the articles, by-laws and unanimous shareholder agreement without charge.[8]

Right to Examine Shareholder List

A shareholder may examine the list of shareholders who are entitled to receive notice of a meeting during the company's usual business hours at its registered office and at the meeting of shareholders for which the list was prepared.[9]

Right to Receive Shareholder List

A shareholder may require the company to furnish a shareholder list[10] within 10 days of payment by the shareholder of a reasonable fee and sending of an affidavit stating the intended uses of the list. The list, which must set out the name and address of each shareholder of the company and the number of shares and series held by each shareholder, may only be used to influence shareholder voting or make an offer to acquire securities of the company, or be used in connection with the affairs of the company.[11] The shareholder may also require that the list include the name and address of anyone who has an option to acquire the company's shares.[12]

DISSENT AND APPRAISAL

When a fundamental change is to be made to the articles of incorporation of a company, or if the company is to be amalgamated, or wishes to transfer substantially all of its assets, undertake a squeeze-out transaction or continue under another jurisdiction, a shareholder has a right to dissent from the proposed action and claim payment of the fair value of her shares.[13] The claim must relate to all of the shares held by the shareholder. These actions, which give rise to a right to dissent, are described in greater detail in the next chapter.

Often called a "dissent and appraisal remedy", it is intended to ensure that minority shareholders are treated fairly by majority shareholders when significant corporate changes are proposed.

In order to exercise this right, the shareholder must send the company a written objection to the resolution being proposed on or before the meeting at which the resolution will be considered. Within 20 days after learning that the resolution has been adopted or after receiving a notice from the company to that effect, the dissenting shareholder must then send the company a written demand for payment of the fair value of the shareholder's shares, followed by the certificates for those shares not more than 30 days later.

The dissenting shareholder is entitled to receive, within 7 days of sending the written demand for payment, a written offer from the company to pay an amount considered by the directors to be fair value for the shares, along with a statement as to how the fair value was determined. Every offer for shares of the same class or series must be on the same terms. The company must pay the shareholder within 10 days after the offer has been accepted.

The dissenting shareholder may not be paid if the company is unable to meet a statutory solvency test. If there are reasonable grounds for believing that the company will be unable to pay its liabilities as they become due, or the realizable value of the company's assets will be less than the aggregate value of its liabilities, the company is prohibited from paying for the shares.

FINANCIAL STATEMENTS

Right to Examine Financial Statements

The shareholder has the right to examine the consolidated financial statements of the company and its subsidiaries during the company's usual business hours and may make extracts free of charge. [14]

Right to Receive Financial Statements

The company is required to send to the shareholders, not less than 21 days before each annual meeting, or before the signing of a resolution in lieu of an annual meeting, the comparative financial statements for the company's latest completed financial year and for the immediately preceding financial year, together with the auditor's report, if any, unless the shareholder has declined to receive them.[15] These statements must also be placed before the shareholders at the meeting.

The statements must be prepared as prescribed by the CBCA regulations and in accordance with Canadian generally accepted accounting principles.[16] They should include at least a balance sheet, statement of retained earnings, income statement, and statement of changes in financial position.

RECEIPT OF COMPANY DIVIDENDS

As mentioned above, every shareholder is entitled to receive any dividend declared by the company if the company has only one class of shares.[17]

However, there is no statutory requirement that a company must declare dividends out of its profits and, to the contrary, there is a statutory prohibition against declaring and paying dividends if the company is unable to meet a test for solvency.[18]

This test will not be met if the company isn't able to pay its liabilities as they become due, or if the realizable value of its assets will be less than the aggregate of its liabilities and the stated capital of its shares. Dividends may be paid by means of fully paid shares of the company or, if it meets this test, in money or property.[19]

Since the decision to declare and pay dividends is made by the company's board of directors in their discretion, a shareholder does not have a right to be paid a dividend unless the dividend has first been declared by the board. Even though the company has earned significant profits and a shareholder wishes that some or all of those profits be paid out as dividends, the directors may prefer to use the profits instead to purchase additional inventory and equipment and hire more staff in order to expand the company's business. They may also decide to retain the profits for future capital expenditures or as a reserve for possible losses. Often, the first thing a board considers when the company's operations are losing money is the reduction or cessation of regular dividends.

However, while a company's dividend policy is normally implemented by the board, the policy may be prescribed by the shareholders in a unanimous shareholder agreement. As discussed in the *Unanimous Shareholder Agreements* chapter, the directors may be required to declare a certain percentage of annual profits as dividends each year, subject to the above solvency test.

A shareholder's right to receive dividends also depends upon the terms of the shares she holds as well as any additional terms in a unanimous shareholder agreement. As discussed in the *Additional Shareholder Rights* chapter, her shares may entitle her to receive preferential, participating and cumulative dividends. Or she may not be entitled to receive any dividends at all, if dividends may be payable to the holders of another class of the company's shares.

RECEIPT OF COMPANY PROPERTY ON DISSOLUTION

If the company has only one class of shares, each shareholder is entitled to receive her share of the remaining property of the company upon its dissolution, as described above.[20] If there is more than one class, the shareholder may not be entitled to receive any property at all, depending upon the terms of her shares. As described in greater detail in the *Additional Shareholder Rights* chapter, her rights on dissolution will be determined by the preferences and other features of her shares.

While shareholders often receive nothing upon the liquidation and dissolution of a company because of payments made to the company's secured and unsecured creditors, the shareholders may be required to reimburse any unpaid creditors and others with valid claims against the company out of any dissolution proceeds which they may receive, provided such claims are brought within two years of the dissolution.[21]

SHARE CERTIFICATES

Right to Receive Share Certificate

Shareholders are entitled to receive at their option either a share certificate or a non-transferable written acknowledgment of their right to obtain such a share certificate from the company. The certificate must be signed by a director or officer of the company or its registrar, transfer agent or trustee, although the signature may be printed or otherwise mechanically reproduced.

Each share certificate should show on its face the name of the company issuing the shares, the name of the shareholder, the number, class and series (if applicable) of the shares represented by the certificate, and a statement that the company is incorporated under the CBCA.

Any restrictions on share transfer, any lien or charge on the shares by the company, and the existence of a unanimous shareholder agreement, should be noted conspicuously on the share certificate, failing which they will be ineffective against any transferee who is unaware of them.

If the company issues shares of more than one class or series, the rights, restrictions and conditions attached to each class or series shall appear on the certificate for such class or series, or a statement that the company will provide the full text of them to the shareholder on request.

If fractional shares arise, perhaps upon a share consolidation or conversion, or an amalgamation of the company with another corporation, the shareholder may receive either fractional certificates or scrip certificates as a result. A scrip certificate entitles the holder to receive a share certificate for a full share by exchanging scrip certificates for fractions totaling a full share. The holder of a fractional certificate may vote and receive dividends only upon a share consolidation or unless the articles so permit, but the holder of a scrip certificate may not vote nor receive dividends.[22]

Right to Receive Replacement Share Certificate

If the shareholder's share certificate has been lost, destroyed or wrongfully taken, the shareholder is entitled to receive a new certificate in place of the original if the shareholder provides an indemnity bond and satisfies any other requirements reasonably imposed by the company.

If, however, the shares represented by the original certificate turn out to have been already transferred to a *bona fide* purchaser, the company may recover the replacement certificate from the shareholder as well as claim against her on the indemnity bond.[23]

SHAREHOLDER MEETINGS

Right to Require Auditor Attendance

Any shareholder, whether entitled to vote or not, may give written notice not less than 10 days before a shareholder meeting to the company's auditor or former auditor to attend the meeting. The auditor or former auditor must then attend the meeting at the company's expense and answer any questions relating to their duties as auditor.[24]

Right to Requisition Meeting

A shareholder, or group of shareholders, holding not less than five per cent of the company's issued voting shares may requisition the directors to call a meeting of shareholders for the purposes stated in the requisition. If the directors do not call a meeting within 21 days of receiving the requisition, any shareholder who signed the requisition may call the meeting.

The shareholders who requisitioned the meeting are entitled to be reimbursed for the expenses reasonably incurred by them in requisitioning, calling and holding the meeting unless the shareholders at the meeting resolve otherwise.[25] Since the majority shareholders have the right to reject any claims for reimbursement by the minority shareholders requisitioning the meeting, the minority shareholders face the risk that they may have to pay their own costs in calling the meeting.

Right to Solicit Proxies

Any person, including an existing shareholder, can solicit proxies from other shareholders to vote their shares at a meeting. So long as the solicitation is not made by or on behalf of the company's management, and so long as it is made to only 15 or fewer shareholders, it can made without the need to prepare and distribute what's called a "dissident proxy circular". Such a circular must be in a prescribed form, and involves considerable time and expense to prepare.[26]

Right to Submit Proposals

Although applicable in practice to more widely-held companies any voting shareholder has the right to submit to the company notice of any matter she would like to propose at an annual meeting of shareholders.[27] The shareholder is entitled to provide a statement in favour of the proposal, which the company is required to include in the management proxy circular for the meeting, if the company solicits proxies, so long as the statement is not more than 500 words.

However, the company is not required to solicit proxies with the notice of meeting if it has just 50 or fewer shareholders entitled to vote.[28] Since a private company for the purposes of this book is defined to have not more than 50 shareholders, a proposal aimed at private company shareholders may not be distributed by the company in advance of the meeting.

Yet the shareholder is still entitled to discuss at any annual meeting any matter on which she would have been entitled to submit a proposal.

The company may request that a proposer show proof of being a shareholder, and refuse to include the proposal if the proposer holds less than 1 per cent of the company's total outstanding voting shares or holds shares worth less than $2,000, or has been a shareholder for fewer than six months.

The company may refuse to include the proposal for a number of additional reasons. For example, if the proposal is not submitted at least 90 days before the anniversary of the date of the company's notice of the last annual meeting. Or if its primary purpose clearly appears to be the enforcement of a personal claim or redress of a personal grievance against the company, or its directors, officers or security holders. Or if it does not relate to the company's business in any significant way, or is being abused to secure publicity. The company can also refuse to include the proposal if a similar proposal was previously submitted to the shareholders and received less than a prescribed minimum amount of support.

The proposal may include nominations for the election of directors at the meeting provided it is signed by the holders of not less than five per cent of the company's outstanding voting shares, although nominations may still be made at the meeting.

If a shareholder makes a proposal to amend the company's articles, the notice of meeting shall set out the proposed amendment and state that any dissenting shareholders shall be entitled to be paid the fair value of their shares in accordance with the dissent and appraisal rights discussed above.[29]

Right to Vote

Unless the company's articles otherwise provide, each share issued by the company entitles its holder to one vote at a shareholder meeting. If the shareholder is a corporation or association, its right to vote may be exercised by any individual authorized by a resolution of the directors or governing body of the corporation or association to vote. If two or more people hold shares jointly, one of them attending the meeting in the absence of the others may vote those shares, but if two or more of them are present, they shall vote their shares as one.[30]

A shareholder entitled to vote may appoint by means of proxy in writing a proxyholder to attend, vote and act at the meeting as the shareholder's nominee to the extent authorized under the proxy.[31] A proxyholder need not be a shareholder. A proxy may be revoked by the shareholder after it is given at any time up to the holding of the meeting or any adjournment.

Although voting may take place by a show of hands unless the company's by-laws otherwise provide, any shareholder or proxyholder may demand that a ballot be taken, either before or after a vote by a show of hands.[32]

The rights of a shareholder to vote can be affected by an agreement she may have signed with other shareholders. Referred to as a "pooling agreement", such an agreement requires that the shares held by the parties be voted in a prescribed manner. It is often used to ensure that all of the shares they hold are voted the same way as a block to maximize their voting power, and can be effective for employee shareholders who want greater influence over company management.[33]

Collective Statutory Shareholder Rights

In contrast to the various individual rights discussed in the previous chapter, there are a number of rights shareholders can exercise collectively in order to accomplish certain things. Ordinarily these rights are exercised at a meeting of company shareholders or by way of a written resolution circulated among all of the shareholders for their signature.

However, any shareholder alone may be able to authorize a particular action through his exercise of these collective rights if he holds a sufficient number of shares to cast either a majority or two-thirds of the votes at a shareholder meeting, depending upon the particular matter.

As with the shareholders' individual rights, these collective rights are, as a general rule, basically shared by all of the shareholders of a private company so long as they are all holders of shares of the same class. However, the holders of different classes may not all have the same collective rights, especially the holders of non-voting shares.

Shareholders generally exercise their collective rights by way of an "ordinary resolution" which entails a simple majority of the votes cast by the shareholders at a meeting on any particular matter. It may also be reflected in a written resolution signed by all of the shareholders who may vote on that matter without holding a meeting.[1] For those companies with only a few shareholders, shareholder approval will usually be obtained by way of a written resolution circulated among the shareholders to avoid the costs and delays normally incurred in sending out notices and holding a shareholder meeting.

However, many of the rights described in this chapter are to be exercised by a "special resolution" of the shareholders, which is a resolution passed by a majority of not less than two-thirds of the votes cast by the shareholders or which is signed by all of the shareholders entitled to vote on the resolution.[2]

Some of the rights to be exercised by special resolution are accompanied by the rights of the holders of a particular class or series to vote separately as a class or series, thereby leading to more than one vote being taken. For example, to amend the articles or approve the transfer of substantially all of the company's assets, approval from each class or series must be given by a special resolution.[3]

AMALGAMATION

If the company proposes to be amalgamated with another corporation, the amalgamation agreement is to be submitted for approval at a meeting of the company's shareholders. Each share, whether voting or non-voting, carries a right to vote in respect of an amalgamation agreement.

The agreement is adopted when it is approved by a special resolution of the company's shareholders. The holders of each class or series of shares are entitled to vote on the agreement as a separate class or series if the agreement provides for amended articles that would give rise to such separate class rights as discussed immediately below under *Amending Articles*.[4]

This right of the shareholders to approve an amalgamation does not apply when the company is being amalgamated with its subsidiary or parent corporation, or with another related subsidiary. Such amalgamations, often referred to as "short form" amalgamations, only require the approval of the directors of the corporations involved.[5]

Since shareholders have dissent and appraisal rights in connection with amalgamations as mentioned in the previous chapter, the special resolution may allow the directors to abandon the amalgamation if difficulties arise from the exercise of such rights.

The company may amalgamate only with another CBCA corporation, although that corporation may have been incorporated under the laws of another jurisdiction and then continued under the CBCA, as described below, just before the amalgamation. An amalgamation of two CBCA corporations does not create a new corporation but rather brings them together as one corporation just as two rivers meet and continue as one river.[6] This is different from the American notion of amalgamation or merger which involves the transfer of assets from a merging corporation into a surviving corporation and then the disappearance of the merging corporation.

Under the CBCA, an amalgamation is a specific procedure involving the consolidation of two or more corporations into one. It is not the same as the sale of assets from one corporation to another, or an exchange of shares among corporations. Upon an amalgamation, the property and liabilities of each amalgamating corporation continue to be the property and liabilities of the amalgamated corporation, including any civil or criminal proceedings or judgments which may be prosecuted or enforced against the amalgamated corporation.[7]

The amalgamation agreement, which the company's shareholders are requested to approve by special resolution, must set out a number of things.[8] It must describe the provisions required to be included in articles of incorporation, such as the corporate name, registered office, share classes, restrictions on share transfer, and the number of directors, along with the names and addresses of those proposed to be directors of the amalgamated corporation. It must specify how shares of the amalgamating companies are to be converted into shares of the amalgamated company.

In addition, the amalgamation agreement must set out what the shareholders are to receive in cash if their shares are not being converted into shares of the amalgamated corporation. It must also state whether the by-laws of the amalgamated corporation will be the same as the by-laws of one of the amalgamating corporations, and if not, it must contain a copy of the proposed by-laws. It must also provide details of any arrangements necessary to complete the amalgamation and provide for the subsequent management and operation of the amalgamated corporation.

In approving the amalgamation agreement, the shareholders should be particularly concerned about the assets and liabilities of the other amalgamating corporation, and whether their shareholding in the amalgamated corporation will be subject to greater risk once the amalgamation takes place, despite the operational synergies that may result. The shareholders should also be concerned that the valuation of each of the amalgamating corporations is reasonably accurate and that the share-exchange ratios provided in the agreement are fair and equitable.

After the amalgamation agreement has been approved by the shareholders of the amalgamating corporations, articles of amalgamation are filed with the Director under the CBCA who must be satisfied that certain facts exist to allow the amalgamation to proceed. Unlike the Director's concern for both creditors and shareholders under a continuance, discussed below, the Director's concern is for the creditors in an amalgamation. The Director does not have the discretionary power to refuse an amalgamation just because it fails to adequately protect the shareholders.[9]

An affidavit from a director or officer of each amalgamating corporation is submitted to the Director which states that the amalgamated corporation will be able to pay its liabilities as they become due, that the realizable value of the amalgamated corporation's assets will not be less than the sum of its liabilities and stated capital of all of its share classes, and that no creditor will be prejudiced by the amalgamation. In addition, the Director may require that a *pro forma* balance sheet for the amalgamated corporation be submitted, and perhaps even require written consent to the amalgamation from certain creditors.

AMENDING ARTICLES

The articles of the company may be amended by a special resolution of the shareholders. Amending the articles may implement a number of changes. The name of the company, the restrictions on the businesses it may carry on, the number of share classes, the rights and restrictions placed on its shares, the minimum and maximum number of its directors, and the restrictions on share transfer, can all be changed by amending the articles.

These items are normally set out in the initial articles when the company is first incorporated. Upon incorporation, the articles, along with the by-laws and any unanimous shareholder agreement, represent the company's charter or "constating documents". Shareholders attempting to understand the company's governance need to be familiar with these documents as well as with the CBCA, and should be aware that a proposed amendment to the articles may significantly affect how the company is governed.

The holders of a class or series of shares may vote separately as a class or series on a proposed amendment if such an amendment will adversely affect the preferences, priorities or rights of their shares, whether or not their class or series is otherwise entitled to vote.[10]

While a number of changes to the articles may be proposed at the same time, it is not necessary to pass a separate special resolution in respect of each change. All the changes may be authorized in one resolution and included in one set of articles of amendment.

AUDITORS

Right to Appoint Auditor

At each annual meeting of shareholders, the shareholders are generally required to appoint by ordinary resolution an auditor to hold office until the close of the next annual meeting.[11] However, the shareholders of a private company (but not of a distributing corporation) may resolve not to appoint an auditor. But that resolution is only valid if unanimously consented to by all of the shareholders, whether they are entitled to vote or not, and even then the resolution is valid only until the next annual meeting.[12]

Right to Remove Auditor

The shareholders may remove the company's auditor by an ordinary resolution at a special meeting unless the auditor was court appointed, and the vacancy then created may be filled at the same meeting.[13]

BY-LAWS

If the directors have made, amended or repealed any by-law, the shareholders are entitled to confirm, reject or amend it at their next shareholder meeting by an ordinary resolution.[14] Any by-law rejected by the shareholders ceases to be effective.

By-laws generally govern the company's internal procedures and are different from resolutions which approve specific acts of the directors or shareholders, such as the declaration of dividends or authorization of a particular contract. Most of the by-laws governing a private company are contained in a comprehensive "general" by-law which is made at the time the company is incorporated and organized, and then amended from time to time thereafter to respond to various changes that may have occurred.

Since the by-laws are part of the company's charter as mentioned above, they have an impact upon how the shareholders are not only able to enforce their rights but also to become aware and participate in the governance of the company should they choose to do so. What follows immediately below is a summary of some of the matters ordinarily addressed in the company's general by-law.

The general by-law is often divided into a number of parts, each part dealing with a separate topic. The first part may address certain operational issues, such as when the company's financial year should end, or who should be authorized to sign company contracts, carry out the company's banking arrangements or vote the company's shares in other corporations. Another part may specify what borrowing may take place and whether security over the company's assets may be given without having to obtain the consent of the shareholders.

The general by-law will set out in another part the various rules applicable to the directors. It will likely stipulate their qualifications to serve, the length of their terms, how they may be elected or removed, and how a vacancy on the board may be filled or additional directors appointed. It may also provide where their meetings are to be held, how meetings are called and notice given, what quorum is required, who may chair a meeting, whether meetings may be held by telephone, how many votes will decide a particular matter, what conflict of interest rules should be observed, and what director remuneration and expense reimbursement may be paid.

Another part may identify the board committees that may be established, and a further part may describe the powers and duties of various officer positions, along with the conflict of interest rules applicable to them. An additional part may stipulate the various circumstances under which a director or officer may be entitled to indemnification by the company for certain losses and expenses incurred, and may provide for the purchase of insurance to support the company's indemnification obligations.

The procedures and conditions relating to the issuance and transfer of company shares may appear in another part of the general by-law. The rules for registration, certificate issuance, joint and deceased shareholders, and any lien for indebtedness to the company may all be prescribed in this part. The rules for the declaration and payment of dividends may be found in another part.

Shareholder meetings will comprise an additional part of the general by-law. How annual and special meetings may be called, where they may take place, whether shareholders may participate by electronic means, who may chair a meeting, who may attend, how joint shareholders are to be treated, the quorum required, and the rules for depositing proxies and voting by proxy, may all be addressed. Furthermore, this part may prescribe the votes to govern a particular matter, the rules for a show of hands and ballots, and how a meeting may be adjourned.

The final part of the general by-law will likely deal with the giving of notices. It may stipulate the acceptable methods for giving notice, how notice periods are calculated, the effect of undeliverable notices, and how joint shareholders are to be notified.

CONTINUANCE

Any application by the company to continue in another corporate jurisdiction, whether provincial or foreign, as if it had been incorporated under the laws of that other jurisdiction must be approved by a special resolution of the company's shareholders. This continuation is often described as an "export" continuance. Each company share carries the right to vote on the continuance whether or not it otherwise carries the right to vote,[15] but there are no separate class votes.

In contrast to an export continuance, an "import" continuance describes a corporation governed by the laws of another jurisdiction continuing under the CBCA. An importing corporation must first satisfy the requirements of its own jurisdiction in authorizing its application for continuance under the CBCA, upon which it may then be discontinued in that jurisdiction.

The special resolution approving an export continuance ordinarily allows the directors to abandon the continuance without further shareholder approval if difficulties arise in the other jurisdiction. Since shareholders have dissent and appraisal rights in connection with export continuances, the special resolution may also allow the directors to abandon the continuance if difficulties arise from the exercise of such rights.

Even if the export continuance is approved by a special resolution of the shareholders, it must still be approved by the Director appointed under the CBCA who must be satisfied that the continuance will not adversely affect the company's creditors or shareholders. The application to the Director should contain an affidavit from a company officer or director stating that the shareholders have received full disclosure of the effect of the continuance on their rights and interests. The application should also contain a statement that the company will honour the rights of dissenting shareholders and that it has adequate funds to pay them.

Where there are complaints by persons who feel they are being adversely affected or oppressed, the Director may refuse the continuance.

DIRECTORS

Right to Elect Directors

At each annual meeting of shareholders, the shareholders are required to elect directors to hold office for a term expiring not later than the close of the third following annual meeting.[16] The election is by ordinary resolution, which usually approves the group of directors or "slate" presented to the meeting. Shareholders may vote in favour of the slate or withhold their vote, but they do not vote against the slate or any particular candidate. They may be able to follow a cumulative voting procedure instead, as described in the *Additional Shareholder Rights* chapter.

Right to Remove Directors

The shareholders may remove any director or directors from office at any special meeting of shareholders, and may fill the resulting vacancy at that meeting. If the holders of any particular class of series of shares have the exclusive right to elect one or more directors, such directors may only be removed by a resolution of those shareholders.[17]

Since the holding of a special meeting may involve some expense to the company, the shareholders may prefer to simply wait until the expiry of the director's term (which is usually at the next annual meeting) and then elect at that meeting another candidate whom the shareholders would rather have as a director.

Right to Restrict Directors' Powers

As part of their rights to amend the articles and confirm the by-laws of the company, the shareholders may authorize various provisions in the articles or by-laws that restrict the powers of the directors.[18] Such restrictions may apply, for example, to the kinds of company business that may be carried on, the issuance and repurchase of shares, the conduct of director meetings, the appointment of officers and their remuneration, and the borrowing of money.

LIQUIDATION AND DISSOLUTION

The shareholders may, by a special resolution, authorize the dissolution of the company or its liquidation and dissolution, provided that the company is not insolvent or bankrupt.[19] If the company has issued more than one class of shares, a special resolution of the holders of each class is required, whether or not they are otherwise entitled to vote.[20]

Upon approval by the shareholders, a statement of intent to dissolve is submitted to the Director appointed under the CBCA. The Director then issues a certificate of intent to dissolve, which starts the liquidation process requiring the company to cease business operations, although the company continues to exist. The company must then notify its creditors, and then proceed to dispose of its properties and discharge its obligations, after which point it may then distribute its remaining property among the shareholders according to their respective rights.

Property that cannot be distributed to shareholders because they cannot be located is to be converted into cash and paid to the Receiver General of Canada.[21] Once the liquidation has been completed, articles of dissolution may be filed with the Director who in turn may issue a certificate of dissolution, upon which the company will cease to exist.

SHAREHOLDER SQUEEZE-OUT

If the company wishes to implement what it is called a "squeeze-out" transaction, the majority of each class of shares affected by the transaction must approve it, voting separately as a class. A squeeze-out involves an amendment to the company's articles, which results in the termination of a shareholder's interest without his consent and without substituting company shares of equivalent value with equal or greater rights.[22]

Approval of the transaction is subject to what is often described as a "majority of the minority" requirement, since those shareholders who will receive after the transaction greater consideration or superior rights or privileges than other shareholders are not entitled to vote. A special resolution of all of the shareholders is also required to approve the amendment to the articles.

Squeeze-out transactions are usually carried out by way of either consolidation of the company's shares or amalgamation with another corporation, and are intended to eliminate a small number of shareholders holding a small number of shares.

Although such transactions result in the expropriation of minority interests, the expropriation is not without compensation, since the minority shareholders are entitled to exercise their dissent and appraisal rights described in the previous chapter. Normally the company or its controlling shareholder will offer a fair price to the shareholders being squeezed-out, given the relatively small percentage of the outstanding shares involved.

In a share consolidation, the outstanding shares are consolidated so that the minority shareholders receive only a fractional interest in a share, which may be eliminated by a cash payment rather than permit the receipt of a fractional certificate. For example, with a consolidation on a 1000 to 1 basis, holders of fewer than 1000 shares would cease to hold shares, leaving a majority shareholder who held more than 1000 shares prior to the consolidation as the only shareholder afterwards. Alternatively, the company may issue scrip certificates for the fractional shares which may be redeemed by the holder for cash within a certain time period. Holders of scrip certificates may not vote or receive dividends.[23]

In an amalgamation squeeze-out, the majority shareholders will transfer their company shares to a newly formed "temporary" corporation which then amalgamates with the company. The amalgamation agreement provides that the holders of all of the company's shares except for the temporary corporation will receive redeemable preferred shares of the amalgamated corporation, whereas the shareholders of the temporary corporation will receive common shares of the amalgamated corporation. The preferred shares are then redeemed, thereby forcing out the original minority shareholders and leaving the company's original majority shareholders as the only shareholders of the amalgamated corporation.

STATED CAPITAL

The company is required to maintain a separate "stated capital" account for each class and series of shares issued. When shares are issued, the full amount of the consideration received by the company for such shares is to be added to the appropriate stated capital account, although less than the full amount may be added in the case of certain transfers between non-arm's length parties, arrangements and amalgamations.[24]

Right to Increase Stated Capital

The shareholders must approve by special resolution any addition to a stated capital account if the amount to be added was not received by the company as consideration for the issuance of shares and the company has at least two classes or series of outstanding shares. An exception exists when there are just two classes outstanding which represent convertible shares.[25]

Right to Reduce Stated Capital

The shareholders may reduce the stated capital of the company by means of a special resolution. Although the stated capital may be reduced for any reason, it is often reduced in order to permit a return of capital to the shareholders, or to reflect a decline in value of the company's realizable assets. This right to reduce the stated capital is subject to a statutory solvency test.[26]

Since a company's capital has traditionally been regarded as a "cushion" for creditors, allowing them to risk possible non-payment of amounts they may be owed by the company, the reduction of capital has certain implications for the company's perceived creditworthiness. A company's capital is more frequently reduced through its purchase or redemption of its outstanding shares.

TRANSFER OF ALL OF THE ASSETS

A sale, lease or exchange of all or substantially all of the property of the company other than in the ordinary course of business requires the approval of the holders of each class or series by way of special resolution. The notice of the meeting requesting approval is to include the agreement for the transaction or a summary of it. Each share of the company carries the right to vote for this purpose whether or not it is otherwise a voting share.

The holders of a particular class or series of shares are entitled to vote separately as a class or series only if their class or series is affected differently by the transaction than another class or series. The shareholders may authorize the directors to fix any of the terms and conditions of the transaction.[27]

In determining whether the property being transferred constitutes substantially all of the company's property in order to require a special resolution, the transfer is to be looked at "qualitatively", assessing whether the nature of the company's business will be fundamentally changed should the property be transferred, and not "quantitatively" by just looking at its value.[28]

Since shareholders have dissent and appraisal rights in connection with the transaction, the special resolution may allow the directors to abandon the transaction without further approval from the shareholders in case problems are created through the exercise of such rights.

Additional Shareholder Rights

In addition to the foregoing rights given in the CBCA to a shareholder to be exercised either individually or collectively, there are a number of other rights a shareholder may acquire either by the terms of the shares she holds or by the terms of a separate agreement. The agreement may be a subscription agreement into which she enters with the company, a share purchase agreement entered into with another shareholder and the company, or even a unanimous shareholder agreement into which she enters with the company and all of the company's shareholders.

Some of these rights may be reflected in both the share terms and a separate agreement. However, because the share terms ordinarily appear in the company's articles, which are on public file, certain rights are better expressed in a private agreement. Depending upon the nature of such rights and the need of the parties for confidentiality, it may not be appropriate for those rights to be inserted in the company's articles and thereby subject to possible public scrutiny.

This chapter discusses some of these additional rights that many shareholders of private companies enjoy. Often these rights come by way of preferred or special shares, which are issued with considerably more features than those associated with ordinary common shares. But some of these rights are enjoyed by common shareholders who have acquired such rights by contract. It is not unusual for just one shareholder, as the only holder of a separate class of shares with many distinctive features, to enjoy many of these rights to the exclusion of all of the other shareholders.

Some of the rights mentioned in this chapter may also be referred to in the *Unanimous Shareholder Agreements* chapter, since such agreements are often used to provide a consolidated source of all of the non-statutory rights and restrictions applicable to a particular company's shareholders. However, this chapter will not discuss the additional rights a shareholder may have for buying and selling company shares, since such rights are discussed exclusively in the next chapter.

CONVERSION RIGHTS

A holder of the company's preferred shares may have the right to convert his preferred shares into common shares of the company. Ordinarily the preferred shares are convertible at the option of the holder at any time. Conversion may be desirable if the company's common shares are likely to receive increasing dividends that exceed the fixed dividend that may be payable on the preferred shares.

However, they may be automatically converted into common shares on a mandatory basis in the event that the company makes an initial public offering or IPO, or if a takeover offer is received to buy a majority of the company's common shares. Because the special voting rights and other terms of preferred shares are often inconsistent with the terms, or absence of terms, for public market securities, the preferred shares may be designed to simply disappear on an IPO through conversion. The size of the IPO that triggers the conversion greatly varies among companies, but the size should be sufficient to create an adequate "float" when the common shares trade publicly.

As part of the conversion, the preferred shareholder may be entitled to payment of all accrued but unpaid dividends, either in cash or shares. In the case of automatic conversion on a takeover offer, a minimum share price might be required.

The rate at which a preferred share is converted into a common share will depend upon a number of factors. It may be based upon the "pre-money valuation" of the company, which is the value of the company before the funds of the preferred shareholder are contributed, and the dollar amount of the funds to be contributed. It may also be based upon the projected value of the company, and the likelihood of the shareholder receiving her desired rate of return in the event of a future sale of her shares in the company.

Determining the conversion rate can become quite complex, especially when later rounds of financing from other investors are anticipated and the percentage ownership of the preferred shareholder is diluted as a result. Generally speaking, the conversion rate of the preferred shares into the company's common shares is calculated by dividing the original purchase price of the preferred shares by a "conversion price" which is initially set at the original purchase price to achieve a 1-to-1 conversion of preferred shares into common shares.

DILUTION PROTECTION RIGHTS

The conversion price is normally adjusted automatically for any stock dividends, combinations or splits, in order that the preferred shares will convert into the number of common shares that will maintain the preferred shareholder's percentage of equity in the company.

However, an adjustment to the conversion price may also take place if the company needs to issue additional equity in subsequent rounds of financing at less than the original purchase price paid for the preferred shareholder's shares. The preferred shareholder may be given the rights to obtain more common shares on conversion, without additional aggregate consideration, in the event that the company subsequently issues new common shares or equivalent securities at a price below the then current conversion price. The conversion price of the preferred shares is effectively decreased, resulting in more common shares per preferred share being issued upon conversion.

This dilution protection is often justified because there is no readily available, independent market price for the company's shares, and the preferred shareholder should be protected against having overpaid. It effectively requires the company's managers holding common shares to pay through dilution if they don't succeed in increasing the value of the company by the next round of financing. From their point of view, however, any decrease in the value of the company could result from events beyond their control. More importantly, such dilution protection may deny the company the flexibility it may need in a downturn to raise new financing at a lower price.

Dilution protection may be afforded to the preferred shareholder in one of two ways. It may use either a "weighted average" formula or a "ratchet" formula. The weighted average formula uses the discounted price and number of the new common shares sold in adjusting the conversion price of the preferred shares downwards. Under this formula, the sale by the company of a large number of common shares at a price slightly lower than the conversion price, and the sale of a small number of common shares at a much lower price, collectively result in a relatively small adjustment to the conversion price of the preferred shares.

The ratchet formula, on the other hand, automatically decreases the conversion price of the preferred shares to the lowest price at which the new common shares have been issued, regardless of the number of new shares issued.

The holders of common shares generally want the weighted average formula to apply if discount stock is offered in the future, given the greater dilution of their shares if the ratchet formula is applied instead. To arrive at a formula, a hybrid of both the weighted average and the ratchet formulas may end up being used, such as applying the ratchet formula for the first two years of the preferred shareholder's investment and the weighted average formula thereafter in an effort to discourage the early issuance of discount stock. Alternatively, the ratchet formula might apply only if the discount stock is issued at a price below a specified threshold price.

There are often certain exceptions to these dilution protection provisions. The most common exception relates to the pool of shares, ranging somewhere between five and 20 per cent of the outstanding fully-diluted shares of the company, which is set aside for issuance to key employees. The size of this pool may be adjusted from time to time to accommodate any future share issuances that have been approved by the preferred shareholder.

DIVIDEND RIGHTS

As described in the *Individual Statutory Shareholder Rights* chapter, every shareholder has a statutory right to receive any dividend declared by the company if the company has only one class of shares, but there is no statutory requirement that a company must declare and pay dividends.

However, the terms of any particular class, or the terms of any particular series, may provide that the holder is entitled to receive a dividend of a certain amount to be paid at certain times. The amount payable may be a specific dollar amount or may be calculated at a prescribed percentage of the amount originally paid for the shares, a percentage which often approximates prevailing interest rates.

Whether or not a company issues shares with rights to prescribed dividends may depend upon the expectations of its shareholders and the financial circumstances of the company. If its shareholders expect to derive most of their financial return in the form of capital appreciation of their shares, they may allow the shares to be dividend-free for a while so that the company's cash flow can be dedicated to funding future growth. However, they may expect that dividends should be payable at a later stage when the company's projected cash flow is strong enough to provide the shareholder with a current, as opposed to a deferred, capital return.

The terms of preferred shares with dividend rights will likely require the company to first pay dividends to the holders of the preferred shares before paying dividends to the holders of the common shares. This preference may apply to the payment of dividends in whatever amount may be declared by the company's board of directors, or apply only to a fixed dollar amount, usually between five to 10 per cent of the original purchase price of the preferred shares, before dividends can be paid on the company's common shares.

In addition to enjoying this preference for dividends, the preferred shareholders may also have a right to further participate in the profits of the company along with the common shareholders. Their shares may require that their dividends be participating, so that they are entitled to receive additional dividends rateably with the holders of the company's common shares once all of the preferences have been satisfied.

Furthermore, the terms of the preferred shares may entitle the holder to receive cumulative as well as preferential and participating dividends, so that unpaid dividends accumulate from year-to-year, and that all cumulative dividends must first be paid to the holders of the preferred shares before dividends can be paid to the holders of the common shares.

These preferential, participating or cumulative dividend requirements aren't necessarily onerous on the company. They place a burden on the company only when it wants to pay dividends to the holders of the common shares, and is prevented from doing so unless it also pays the holders of the preferred shares. However, a heavy burden can be placed upon the company if the preferred shares require mandatory cumulative dividends, requiring the company to accumulate and make periodic dividend payments on those shares. Such a requirement may not be enforceable, however, depending upon the ability of the company to satisfy the dividend solvency test described in the *Individual Statutory Shareholder Rights* chapter.

INFORMATION RIGHTS

A shareholder may be entitled, perhaps under a subscription agreement or unanimous shareholder agreement, to receive ongoing financial information directly from the company on a regular basis and not simply by way of her nominee director at board meetings, if she is entitled to nominate a director at all. The information to be provided usually includes monthly or quarterly management financial statements and audited annual financial statements. Other information generally to be provided includes management budgets, forecasts and variance reports, along with research and development reports and certificates from the chief financial officer that all statutory deductions have been appropriately withheld and remitted.

The shareholder may also be granted ongoing inspection and audit rights, which permit her to visit and inspect the company's properties, examine the company's accounts and records, and discuss the company's affairs and finances with company officers. The company may, however, qualify such rights by excluding the provision of any information it reasonably believes to be trade secrets or other confidential information unless it is satisfied with the confidentiality arrangements made with the inspecting parties.

LIQUIDATION RIGHTS

Although a preferred shareholder may not succeed in obtaining early redemption rights as discussed below, she is almost always entitled to a preference over the common shareholders in getting her investment back in the event that the company is liquidated, either upon insolvency or a sale of substantially all of the company's assets.

After payment is made out of the liquidation proceeds to secured and unsecured creditors, payment must then be made to the preferred shareholders before any payment can be made to the company's common shareholders. The amount of the preferential payment to be made is usually set at the original purchase price of the preferred shares, adjusted for any stock dividends, combinations or splits. There may be an obligation to increase this amount by including any accrued but unpaid dividends, or, in the absence of the right to receive cumulative dividends, by providing a guaranteed return of perhaps between five and 10 per cent of the original purchase price.

In addition to receiving this preferential amount, the preferred shareholder may be entitled to participate rateably in the distribution of the company's remaining proceeds of liquidation with the common shareholders. Sometimes the common shareholders are permitted to receive back their own purchase price first before the preferred shareholders participate with the common shareholders in the remaining proceeds.

The liquidation preference enjoyed by the preferred shareholder may have to be subordinated in a subsequent round of financing undertaken by the company, so that new investors will have a senior position on liquidation or at least rank equally with the preferred shareholder. In such circumstances, liquidation may include the acquisition of the company or its merger with another corporation.

NOMINATION RIGHTS

The shareholders may be quite prepared to leave the directors and officers free to operate the company on a day-to-day basis so long as the company is complying with its budgets and business plans and meeting any specific objectives or milestones that have been agreed upon. However, a shareholder may be given the right, perhaps in a unanimous shareholder agreement, to nominate one or more directors to the company's board, or at least be given the right to have a nominee attend board meetings as an observer.

Observers are usually entitled to receive notice of and to attend meetings of the board of directors, but are not entitled to vote. Shareholders comprised of venture capital and private equity firms often prefer to limit the involvement of their nominees to observer status if the board already consists of nominees of other professional investors, or as a way of avoiding director liability or the policies of certain stock exchanges which place escrow requirements during an initial public offering on shareholders having board representation.

A shareholder may have further rights to nominate persons to serve on certain board committees as well as occupy specific management positions. A more comprehensive description of shareholder nomination rights, how they are exercised and how they may change, is provided in the *Unanimous Shareholder Agreements* chapter in its discussion of board and management representation.

PRE-EMPTIVE RIGHTS

The articles may provide the shareholders with the right to acquire their proportionate share of any new shares which the company intends to issue.[1] If this pre-emptive right is contained in the articles, the new shares must be offered to the shareholders in proportion to their current holdings at the same price and on the same terms at those offered to others. While pre-emptive rights provide the shareholders with some protection against dilution of their equity interest in the company, such rights may hinder the company's ability to raise additional capital and may not be appropriate in every circumstance.

However, even if such rights are provided in the articles, the shareholders have no pre-emptive rights for shares issued for other than money or as dividends, or as part of the exercise of previously granted options or conversion privileges.

Pre-emptive rights are described in greater detail in the *Unanimous Shareholder Agreements* chapter, including the procedures to be followed in their exercise, since such agreements usually contain pre-emptive rights provisions.

REDEMPTION RIGHTS

Preferred shares can be made redeemable by either the company, in calling the shares for repurchase, or by the holder, in putting the shares to the company to receive cash back. This right of the shareholder to redeem is often called a "retraction" right to distinguish it from the company's redemption right.

It is not unusual for a shareholder to be able to insist that the company redeem her preferred shares under certain conditions, if she so elects. The redemption price is normally comprised of the original purchase price of her preferred shares, adjusted for any stock dividends, combinations or splits, plus all accrued and unpaid dividends, and, in many cases, a redemption premium.

Mandatory redemption by the company on specified dates or upon specified events, however, is not generally prescribed since it deprives the company of the flexibility it may need to address its future capital needs. Mandatory redemption also discourages other investors from participating in future rounds of company financing and can make it difficult for the company to obtain bank loans and trade credit.

While redemption at the option of the company may apply to all shares of a class at the same time, provision is often made for the redeemed shares to be selected by lot if not all are redeemed at once. Alternatively, they may be redeemed in proportion to the number of shares held by each shareholder.

Although the conditions under which a company may be required to redeem the preferred shares at the shareholder's option are far from standard, redemption is often permitted only after a sufficiently long period has elapsed, usually around five years. Payment upon such redemption is often required to be made in instalments spread out over a number of months or even years. However, redemption may be accelerated in the event of a sale of a majority of the company's shares, or an initial public offering.

As an alternative to, or in addition to, prescribing redemption rights for the preferred shares, the shareholder might be provided with a "put" giving her the right, after a certain period of time if no other event permitting redemption has occurred, to sell her shares back to the company at a price equal to their fair market value as determined by an outside appraiser or upon application of a prescribed formula.

However, whether provided as puts or rights of redemption, these terms can be of limited practical value should the company be unable to pass the solvency test imposed under the CBCA.

Specifically, the directors of the company are prohibited from repurchasing the company's shares if there are reasonable grounds for believing the company is, or after payment for the shares will be, unable to pay its liabilities as they become due, or if the realizable value of the company's assets will then be less than the aggregate of its liabilities and stated capital of all classes. A similar prohibition applies to the redemption of the company's shares, although the realizable value of the company's assets must not be less than the aggregate of its liabilities and the amount it has to pay to the holders of other shares before or rateably with the holders of the shares being redeemed.[2]

In order to give the holders of preferred shares some comfort that their shares will be redeemed, the shares may require the company to establish a purchase or "sinking" fund to be maintained and used for the purchase and redemption of the company's shares. Such a fund is normally established when the preferred shares are designed to be outstanding for a number of years before redemption. To avoid having to make a large payment at the end of this period, the fund may provide for the mandatory retirement of a certain number of shares at regular intervals before maturity, allowing for the gradual decrease in the number of preferred shares outstanding.

REGISTRATION RIGHTS

It's possible that a shareholder may be given what are called "registration" rights if the company is likely to become eligible to list on NASDAQ or other American exchanges. These rights allow the shareholder to "demand" that the company qualify the shareholder's shares in the company for public distribution in the United States, and thereby dictate the timing of a public offering. They also provide the shareholder with "piggyback" rights under which her shares are to be included in any "primary" registration, when the company files a registration statement to permit the sale of its shares from treasury, or in any "secondary" registration, when the company files a registration statement to permit other shareholders to sell.

Demand registration rights ordinarily entitle the shareholder to require the company to register the company's shares after a certain period of time, usually three to five years, with the United States Securities and Exchange Commission by filing a registration statement. The number of permissible "demands" varies, but the shareholder is normally entitled to at least two.

Granting a shareholder demand registration rights can place a significant burden on the company given the time and cost involved if those rights are exercised. All expenses incurred in demand registrations are normally paid by the company. In practice, exercising the demand doesn't necessarily mean that a public offering will happen. Since the company's management has to go on the "road show" and make convincing presentations to the fund managers and brokers who will be buying the company's shares, management can usually resist the demand to register if business conditions are not favourable.

Piggyback registration rights obligate the company to use its best efforts to include the shareholder's shares in any public registrations the company intends to make. However, such rights are always subject to the underwriter's discretion to exclude the shareholder's shares from the offering. Such rights are also usually excluded from any offering of shares in the context of a corporate acquisition or employee stock option or purchase plan.

VETO RIGHTS

In addition to having nomination rights, a shareholder may be able to participate in important management matters by exercising certain veto rights. These matters generally include operating budgets, major capital expenditures, executive hiring and firing, compensation levels, equity and debt financings, material strategic alliances, larger acquisitions and sales, dividend payments, share redemptions, and other significant actions out of the ordinary course of the company's business.

The shareholder may have effective control over these particular matters by being able to vote on them as a separate class, or through the use of super-majority voting rules at the board level if she or her nominee is a director, or simply through a requirement that her written consent must be obtained. Whatever mechanism is chosen, she may have the right to veto the implementation of any of these matters.

These veto rights are described in greater detail in the *Unanimous Shareholder Agreements* chapter in its discussion of major decisions.

VOTING RIGHTS

While a shareholder's basic voting rights have already been outlined in the *Individual Statutory Shareholder Rights* chapter, she may have a number of additional voting rights, or perhaps multiple voting rights, or merely different or restricted voting rights. She may also have no right to vote at all except in those circumstances prescribed by statute as outlined in that chapter and in the *Collective Statutory Shareholder Rights* chapter. Or her right to vote may arise only upon the occurrence of a specific event, such as the failure to pay a cumulative dividend for a certain period of time.

Shareholders with convertible preferred shares are ordinarily granted the same number of votes as the votes carried by the common shares into which the preferred shares are convertible, generally on a one vote per share basis.

Yet some classes of shares may give the holders a number of votes per share, not just one vote. It is not unusual for a group of related shareholders, often members of the same family along with their personal holding corporations and family trusts, to hold all of the shares of one class which permits five or 10 votes for each share. By holding the class with multiple voting rights, the related shareholders may be able to outvote the holders of other classes with "inferior" or "subordinate" voting rights even though their equity interest in the company is smaller than the equity interests of the other shareholders. Furthermore, employee shareholders are often issued shares with subordinate voting rights.

To allow a shareholder to carry out some of the additional rights described in this chapter, such as the right to elect directors or veto certain company decisions, her shares may allow her to vote as a separate class.

The shareholder may also get the benefit of "cumulative voting" in the election of directors, which gives her the right to cast a number of votes equal to the number of voting shares she holds, multiplied by the number of directors to be elected. She may then cast all such votes in favour of one candidate or distribute them among the various candidates in any proportion she chooses. This type of voting enables those holding just a minority of company shares to elect one or more directors. Cumulative voting is permitted under the CBCA.[3]

WITHDRAWAL OR LOSS OF RIGHTS

Although this chapter describes some of the additional rights a shareholder may acquire by contract or under the terms of her shares, she may be forced to lose such rights if she declines to invest additional funds when required later on or if her equity holdings in the company fall below a specified percentage.

For example, a preferred shareholder may lose her dilution protection, and perhaps her liquidation preference and right to nominate directors, if she fails to make an investment in any future company financing in proportion to her current percentage holdings. Such a "pay-to-play" provision encourages future investment and assistance by the shareholder in helping the company to grow. A pay-to-play provision generally forces a shareholder failing to participate in a future financing to convert her preferred shares into common shares or into a series of preferred shares lacking price-based dilution protection. Alternatively, she may simply be required to waive any dilution adjustments she might otherwise be entitled to as a preferred shareholder.

Sometimes a shareholder's veto rights as well as her information rights may disappear once her equity ownership in the company is reduced below a certain percentage.

Buy-Sell Rights

As mentioned in the *Introduction*, the main characteristics which differentiate a private company from a distributing corporation are the restrictions against share transfer, ordinarily found in the articles of incorporation of the private company. These restrictions generally limit the number of shareholders, prevent share transfers without, for example, approval by a majority of directors or shareholders, and prohibit solicitations to the public to subscribe for company securities.

These restrictions against transfer are not the only reason private company shares are often regarded as illiquid or non-marketable. Because there is no public market for them, there may not be any market for them at all. Consequently, anyone acquiring the shares of a private company tries to determine at the outset whether he will be able to find a buyer when he eventually wants to sell them. He may want to ensure that he has some contractual protection against being stuck with shares nobody else wants.

A buy-sell agreement, or more likely a unanimous shareholder agreement containing buy-sell provisions, can provide the shareholder with this kind of contractual protection. It may give him an exit, or prescribe a "liquidity event", which may permit him to get some or all of his investment back, perhaps with an extra return as well. Because a unanimous shareholder agreement is an agreement between all of the shareholders, the share transfers required or permitted under the agreement are deemed to have received shareholder approval in compliance with any transfer restrictions in the company's articles.

A unanimous shareholder agreement often includes provisions relating to the transfer of company shares to persons outside the existing shareholder group, including rights of first refusal, piggyback rights and drag-along rights, which are described below. It also includes transfers within the existing shareholder group when certain events take place, such as the death, disability or termination of employment of a shareholder. Some transfers are mandatory, whereas other transfers are optional.

This chapter describes the provisions ordinarily found in a unanimous shareholder agreement that deal with the rights and obligations of the shareholders and the company relating to the transfer of the company's shares, although they may also be found in separate buy-sell agreements. However, the shareholders' rights and obligations relating to the issuance of company shares are described instead in the *Unanimous Shareholder Agreements* chapter in its discussion of pre-emptive rights and mandatory shareholder funding.

FIRST REFUSAL RIGHTS

A shareholder may be given a right of first refusal on the transfer of any company shares proposed by any other shareholders in the future. In contrast to pre-emptive rights, which are intended to maintain a shareholder's percentage of equity ownership in the company, rights of first refusal are intended to increase his equity ownership in the company in the event that any of the other shareholders decides to sell. As with pre-emptive rights, rights of first refusal often apply to any shares, or securities exchangeable or convertible into shares, including rights, options or warrants, and not just to shares of the same class as are already held by the shareholder.

Exemptions from rights of first refusal are ordinarily given for transfers to a registered retirement savings plan or other trust of which the shareholder is the beneficial owner, or to a shareholder's spouse, or to a shareholder's personal holding corporation provided that the shareholders of the holding corporation agree not to transfer their shares in the holding corporation unless they concurrently transfer the shares of the company to another exempt party.

In the case of corporate shareholders, exemptions from rights of first refusal may be available to cover transfers to affiliates. In the case of shareholders who are investment managers, exempt transfers might include transfers to other funds or corporations they manage.

A transfer that is exempt from rights of first refusal is often specifically permitted in the unanimous shareholder agreement and may take place despite the general restrictions against transfers of the company's shares.

The events that specifically trigger the right of first refusal often vary. Some unanimous shareholder agreements require that a "bona fide offer" must be received by the selling shareholder for all of his shares from a third party before notice is to be given to the other shareholders of their rights to purchase such shares. They are then entitled to purchase a percentage of the shares equal to their percentage ownership of the company, at the same price and on the same terms as the third party offer. If the other shareholders do not take up all of the shares, the selling shareholder may then sell all of his shares to the third party at the price and on the terms of the original offer. In order to prevent any disputes over the value of non-cash consideration, the agreement usually provides that the price in the original offer be paid in cash on closing. It also usually provides that upon closing, the third party purchaser must become a party to the agreement.

Obviously this requirement deters potential third party purchasers from incurring the time and expense involved in preparing a serious offer which may be ignored if any one of the other shareholders elects to exercise his purchase rights. It does, however, benefit the existing shareholders by letting them know the identity of their prospective fellow shareholder and effectively giving them a veto over him. Perhaps more significantly, it gives them some indication of the fair value of the shares being offered to them, assuming the third party is acting at arm's-length with the selling shareholder.

As an alternative, the agreement may provide what is commonly called a "right of first offer", which permits the selling shareholder to simply give notice to the other shareholders of his intention to sell at a price and on such terms as he chooses. They are then entitled to purchase a percentage of his shares equal to their percentage ownership of the company, but if they don't, he may then sell his shares to a third party provided the price and terms are no more favourable than those originally offered to the other shareholders.

While this alternative helps the selling shareholder to set a minimum price that he can subsequently use in negotiating with third parties, it may encourage the selling shareholder to specify an inflated price with the expectation that the other shareholders will elect to purchase at that price rather than risk a third party becoming a shareholder. Furthermore, if the other shareholders have decided not to purchase the offered shares, it affords them no opportunity to prevent the selling shareholder from selling to a third party whom they might regard as an undesirable shareholder. This latter concern, however, may be addressed by incorporating into the agreement a list of prohibited third party purchasers, which might include any competitors of the company or of the current shareholders.

Deciding which of these two alternatives is preferable for inclusion in the unanimous shareholder agreement requires the shareholders to weigh their desire for the potential liquidity of their shares against their desire to control who may become a new shareholder.

Despite the inclusion of any first refusal rights, the agreement may contain a prohibition against any share transfers to third parties for a certain period of time. Sometimes referred to as a "standstill" provision, it can be used to keep all of the current shareholders working together to promote the success of the company's business, perhaps during a crucial start-up phase.

Under most rights of first refusal, the selling shareholder is required to offer all, but not less than all, of his shares to the other shareholders. Furthermore, once the other shareholders have declined to buy all of his shares, the selling shareholder is usually required to close his sale to the third party within a certain period of time, failing which the first refusal process has to start all over again. Rights of first offer may permit a longer time period, since the third party negotiations may not start until after all of the current shareholders have declined. However, the longer the time period, the greater the chance that the offer price will cease to reflect the current value of the shares because of intervening material changes to the company's business.

PIGGYBACK RIGHTS

A shareholder may be entitled to participate in another shareholder's proposed sale of company shares, usually when the sale results in a change of control of the company or involves a substantial percentage of outstanding shares. Intended to enhance the liquidity of minority shareholdings, many unanimous shareholder agreements allow a shareholder to "piggyback" on a third party offer made to a majority shareholder.

A piggyback provision often applies when a shareholder or group of shareholders with a majority of the company's shares has complied with the rights of first refusal requirements and proposes to sell to a third party. He may proceed to sell his shares to the third party so long as he has caused the third party to offer to purchase the shares of the other shareholders at the same price and on the same terms.

The agreement may provide "co-sale" rights instead. Unlike piggyback rights, which allow minority shareholders to have all of their shares included in a third party purchase offer, co-sale rights provide for the inclusion of only such portion of their shares which, when added to the portion held by the majority shareholders, equals the number of shares which the third party wishes to purchase. The number of shares that the majority can sell is effectively reduced and replaced by the number of shares that the minority shareholders elect to sell to the third party. In the event that the third party wishes to purchase all of the company's outstanding shares, the difference between piggyback rights and co-sale rights disappears in practice.

While rights of first refusal generally prohibit third party offers from consisting of non-cash consideration, piggyback rights, and drag-along rights discussed below, often permit non-cash consideration to be part of third party offers.

DRAG-ALONG RIGHTS

A minority shareholder may also be required to participate in a sale of company shares by a majority shareholder. His own shares may be "dragged along" as a way of increasing the marketability of the majority shareholder's shares since a third party purchaser may be more likely to want all of the shares of the company rather than have to deal with other company shareholders after the purchase.

A drag-along provision is effectively the reverse of a piggyback provision. It provides that if a third party makes an offer to purchase all of the shares of the company, those shareholders holding a majority or perhaps higher percentage of the company's shares who wish to accept the offer may require the other shareholders to sell their shares to the third party at the same price and on the same terms, so long as the right of first refusal provisions have first been complied with.

This provision allows the majority shareholder to market 100 per cent of the company's shares and obtain the maximum sale price from a purchaser who is prepared to pay a higher price for all of the shares than he would pay for just majority control.

Because of the requirement for "majority of the minority" approval to complete a squeeze-out transaction as discussed in the *Collective Statu-*

tory Shareholder Rights chapter, and the possible difficulty in obtaining such approval, the drag-along provision in a unanimous shareholder agreement is often viewed as a more effective way to eliminate minority positions in a private company.

TRANSFER RIGHTS UPON CERTAIN EVENTS

A shareholder may be able to require the other shareholders to buy his shares upon the occurrence of certain events. Alternatively, the shareholder may be required to sell his shares to the others upon the occurrence of the same events. The death of the shareholder, if the shareholder is an individual, is the event specified in most unanimous shareholder agreements as requiring a share transfer. Other events triggering such a requirement include the termination of a shareholder's employment with the company, whether voluntary or involuntary, the shareholder's disability, bankruptcy or insolvency, or a breach of a material provision of the agreement.

These requirements usually appear as a number of "puts" and "calls" in the agreement. A put, or option to sell, gives a shareholder a right, but not an obligation, to sell his shares either to the company or to other shareholders upon the prescribed events. As the opposite of a put, a call gives a shareholder or the company a right, but again not an obligation, to buy the shares of another shareholder.

However, instead of structuring the requirements as a series of puts and calls, some agreements provide for mandatory, not optional, purchases. This approach is often thought to be desirable in the event of death or disability of the shareholder since the shares will have a ready buyer.

Most agreements require a shareholder to sell his shares when a call is exercised after a prescribed event. Yet they often vary over which party may exercise the call and purchase his shares. Some agreements give call rights to the company, some give them to just a majority shareholder or group of shareholders, while others give them to all of the shareholders based upon their percentage holdings of company shares.

Although selecting the company as the buyer may appear to be the easiest approach to take, it may result in undesirable consequences – apart from considerations of whether or not the company will have the funds available to pay for the shares.

For example, a company redemption or repurchase may well have negative tax implications for the selling shareholder.[1] Also, the proportionate voting rights of the other shareholders and voting control could be altered upon the cancellation of that shareholder's shares. Furthermore, the redemption or repurchase could possibly cause the company to be in default under the negative covenants in its financing agreements, or perhaps be in contravention of the statutory solvency test for the redemption or purchase of its shares discussed in the *Additional Shareholder Rights* chapter.

In light of these possible consequences, the agreement may provide that if the company is unable to buy the shares, then another shareholder or group of shareholders shall buy the shares instead.

The treatment of an employee's shares upon termination of employment often depends upon how and why the termination takes place. If it is "for cause", the company is likely to be given a call option to purchase the employee's shares, whereas the employee is likely to be given a put option to sell his shares if he is terminated without cause. If the employee simply resigns, the company can usually call the employee's shares.

VALUATION OF TRANSFERRED SHARES

Even though the shareholders may be able to agree upon the various puts and calls to be exercised in respect of their shares, they may have some difficulty in deciding which method should be used to value their shares when these options are exercised. Since there is no readily available market for determining their value, the unanimous shareholder agreement must provide some valuation guidance. Whether a share purchase is mandatory or optional, the agreement usually specifies one of two ways to arrive at a purchase price for the shares being purchased.

One approach the agreement may adopt is the requirement to apply a particular formula. Even then, there are different formulas from which to choose. The agreement may select an asset-based method, such as net book value or appraised asset value. Or it may select an earnings-based method, perhaps using discounted cash flow or a multiple of earnings. Or it may select a specific industry rule of thumb, such as a dollar value per existing customer.

The other approach involves the retention of a professional business valuator to determine the value of the shares to be sold. The agreement will often specify who the valuator should be and who should pay the valuator's fees. It may also provide some general rules for the valuator regarding which valuation methods should be used or avoided, and which assumptions and adjustments ought to be made. For example, it may stipulate that no control premium or minority discount is to be considered, but that the goodwill associated with a departing shareholder may be taken into account.

Each approach has its advantages and disadvantages. But while they both afford the parties a mechanism for valuation, they don't guarantee either certainty or fairness of result. The formula approach tends to be the easier and faster one, but may not be suitable for every company. For example, a decision to use book and not appraised asset values, or a multiple of recent earnings and not a discount of projected earnings, may appear misguided in hindsight and create resentment.

By taking the valuator approach, assuming that all the parties can agree upon a choice of valuator, the valuator chosen may turn out to be more expensive and take much longer to perform the valuation than the parties originally expected. Often the closing date prescribed in the agreement becomes unworkable because of delays in receiving the valuator's report. If the agreement names the company's auditor as the valuator, the auditor may have difficulty reconciling the conflicts between audit and valuation duties. It's usually preferable for an independent party to be named as valuator, and for any closing date to be a specified number of days following delivery of the valuation.

SHOTGUN RIGHTS

Another provision involving the transfer of shares between shareholders is the "shotgun", which has its own particular valuation mechanism. Some unanimous shareholder agreements, normally between just two shareholders, will contain a shotgun provision to provide a means of resolving a possible deadlock between the two shareholders.

A shotgun essentially permits one shareholder to set a price at which he is willing to either sell his shares to the other shareholder, or buy the shares of the other shareholder. Once the shareholder has given notice of the shotgun price, the other shareholder then has to decide which of the two alternatives to accept. Many shotguns require the other shareholder to decide within a relatively short time period, often less than 30 days, and his failure to do so requires him to sell his shares at the price set.

While some shotguns then require payment of the entire purchase price after another relatively short period, again often under 30 days, some provide for payment in regular instalments over as long as 3 or 5 years. The tight time frames dictated by the agreement can certainly work to the disadvantage of the other shareholder, who may have great difficulty in arranging suitable financing within the permitted time should he wish to buy. His ability to pay on time effectively determines whether he buys or sells.

For this reason, shotguns are often only used when there are just two equal shareholders with roughly comparable financial resources. Although shotguns impose an obvious deterrent on the offering shareholder against setting a price that is too high or too low, such deterrence breaks down when the other shareholder lacks financial strength. When that is the case, the attempt to give some certainty to the exit process by adding a shotgun clause is then made at the expense of fairness, because a low ball price becomes inevitable. The financially stronger shareholder will simply take advantage of the other.

Consequently, shotguns may be inappropriate for many companies and shareholders. For start-up and early stage companies that need to keep their shareholders committed, as well as patient for a payback on whatever time and effort has been invested, shotguns are often exercisable only after a period of two years or more has elapsed.

For those companies with shotgun provisions in their unanimous shareholder agreements, such provisions are infrequently exercised. Since shareholders appear reluctant to risk the consequences in practice, shotguns may reflect mutual deterrence. They may actually motivate deadlocked shareholders to negotiate a resolution to a problem rather than pull the trigger. In other words, the main benefit to having a shotgun in place is the threat of its use, not the use itself.

AUCTION RIGHTS

Although not commonly found in unanimous shareholder agreements, shareholders may be given the right to initiate an auction for the company's outstanding shares. The right to hold an auction is usually provided as additional to, and sometimes as an alternative to, some of the rights described in this chapter.

As an alternative to the rights of first refusal, an auction may be chosen by the shareholders as providing the means for the sale of one shareholder's shares to the other shareholders. The auction gives the other shareholders an opportunity to buy a shareholder's shares but does not ensure that they will pay no more than a third party will pay. The auction procedures may require that all of the interested bidders attend at a certain location at a specified time and that a named auctioneer will conduct the auction in accordance with the rules set out in the agreement, with the highest bidder winning.

An auction may also be used instead of the right to exercise a shotgun. The shareholders, especially if there are more than two, may have the right under a unanimous shareholder agreement to initiate an auction for the company's outstanding shares. In this case, the auction procedures may prescribe that each shareholder is to make a sealed bid to buy all of the shares of the company and the shareholder with the highest bid wins.

Unanimous Shareholder Agreements

A unanimous shareholder agreement is an agreement among all of the company's shareholders, both voting and non-voting, which restricts the powers of the directors. It is specifically authorized by the CBCA[1] and is often used to allow a private company to operate much like a partnership but with limited liability. The shareholders can be empowered to run the company in the same way as partners run a partnership.

To qualify as a unanimous shareholder agreement, it must to some extent restrict the powers of the directors to manage, or supervise the management of, the business and affairs of the company. It thereby effectively transfers to the shareholders some or all of the rights, duties and liabilities of the directors. Although agreements to fetter the discretion of company directors have traditionally not been permitted under common law[2], the CBCA allows the shareholders to take away that discretion by means of a unanimous shareholder agreement.

In the absence of a unanimous shareholder agreement, the ability of shareholders to control a private company is generally limited in practice to their power to elect and dismiss directors despite the numerous other rights itemized elsewhere in this book. It is the directors who have the fundamental power and duty[3] to manage the company unless restricted by a unanimous shareholder agreement.

Sometimes viewed as a hybrid concept[4] under corporate law, a unanimous shareholder agreement is part contractual and part constitutional in nature. It must be a written agreement among all of the shareholders of the company, or among all of the shareholders and other parties.[5] As a contract, it governs the personal rights of the shareholders. As a component of the company's constitution, it governs the overall management of the company, including the issuing of shares, passing of by-laws, and appointment of officers. It can also set higher standards than those required under the CBCA, such as the number of votes of directors or shareholders needed to approve any action.[6]

If a unanimous shareholder agreement is in place for a private company, any person acquiring the company's shares is deemed to be a party to it. If certificates are issued for the company's shares and do not conspicuously note or refer to the agreement, the agreement may be ineffective against a transferee who has no actual knowledge of it.[7]

A declaration by the only shareholder of a company which restricts the powers of the company's directors to manage is deemed to be a unanimous shareholder agreement.[8] Such a declaration is often used by foreign corporations wishing to maintain managerial control over their wholly-owned Canadian subsidiaries.

While a shareholder who is a party to a unanimous shareholder agreement acquires some or all of the rights, powers, duties and liabilities of the directors, including any defences available to the directors, the directors are relieved of their rights, powers, duties and liabilities to the same extent.[9] However, while the directors may be relieved of their liabilities under the CBCA, including their obligation[10] for six months' wages remaining unpaid to the company's employees, such relief may not extend to all liabilities, including those imposed on directors by provincial legislation (even though it is unlikely a court will make a director liable for a company's conduct over which she has no control).

This chapter discusses some of the rights, powers and duties otherwise performed by directors which are often assumed by shareholders pursuant to a unanimous shareholder agreement. It also discusses some of the restrictions that are often imposed upon shareholders and some of the rules for governance and financing of the company's business which are normally found in such an agreement.

However, this chapter does not discuss certain additional shareholder rights that are usually contained in a unanimous shareholder agreement because they have already been discussed in the *Additional Shareholder Rights* chapter. Furthermore, while this chapter discusses the provisions relating to the issuance of company shares, it does not discuss those relating to the transfer of company shares, even though such provisions are usually covered in a unanimous shareholder agreement. They were discussed instead in the previous chapter, *Buy-Sell Rights*. Nor does it discuss the dispute resolution procedures which the shareholders may set out in the agreement, since they are discussed in the *Dispute Resolution and Remedies* chapter.

All of these provisions in the agreement, which represent something other than restrictions on the directors' powers, can sometimes cause confusion over whether the agreement actually qualifies as a unanimous shareholder agreement. But so long as the agreement is signed by all of the company's shareholders and restricts the powers of the directors to some extent, its inclusion of other items such as the rights of shareholders to acquire each other's shares or their obligations to finance company operations does not disqualify the agreement as a unanimous shareholder agreement.

REASONS FOR AN AGREEMENT

There are a variety of reasons for the shareholders of a private company to have a unanimous shareholder agreement.

If there is one shareholder holding a majority of the company's shares, the minority shareholders may want to ensure that they have a minimum number of seats on the board of directors so that they will have access to inside information and be able to participate in important decisions in the same way as the majority shareholder.

If the company shareholders represent a number of different and possibly conflicting interests, such as venture capitalists, employees and founding owners, the agreement may provide certain voting mechanisms for protecting their separate interests while reinforcing the different roles they play in ensuring the continuing success of the company's business.

If the business does not permit the company to consistently obtain financing from conventional outside sources, it may be necessary to use the agreement to prescribe how additional capital is to be obtained from the shareholders themselves.

If the company has implemented an employee share ownership plan, an agreement may provide for rights to purchase the shares of an employee who has died or resigned, or has become disabled or been terminated.

An agreement may also be required to provide a buy-sell process for resolving certain disputes between two shareholders operating the company's business as a joint venture. The agreement may also stipulate the winding-up of the joint venture after a certain period of time and the division of its assets among the joint venturers.

Often the shareholders will anticipate problems that might arise in the future and then use the agreement to implement certain practices to deter such problems from arising at all. Some of these problems relate to control and management, others relate to financing and conflicts of interest, while others relate to the possible abuse of power by the majority shareholder. The following represent some of the provisions generally used to address such problems.

BOARD AND MANAGEMENT REPRESENTATION

One of the ways minority shareholders can assert greater control over the management of the company is to insist upon guaranteed board representation. The unanimous shareholder agreement may provide that each shareholder, or related group of shareholders, has the right to nominate a number of directors which is roughly proportional to their shareholdings. This may allow a group with similar interests, perhaps a group of individual employees or financial investors, to have their respective representatives appointed to the board. The agreement may also provide that when the percentage shareholdings of the group changes, their right to board representation correspondingly changes.

The agreement will usually require that all of the shareholders vote in favour of the election of the prescribed nominees to the board of directors and to fill any vacancy on the board with the nominee of the shareholder who was represented by a vacating director. The shareholders will also be required to remove any nominee director who contravenes or votes against the wishes of the shareholder nominating her. A related provision may limit the number of directors so that the right to nominate directors is equal to the right to control a specified portion of the board.

The agreement may require that audit and compensation committees of the board be established, comprised solely of directors unrelated to a majority shareholder or current management, and that directors' and officers' liability insurance be put into place. It may also require that board meetings be held quarterly, if not more frequently, and that the board's quorum rules not allow such meetings to proceed in the absence of certain nominee directors.

To ensure that the company's key management positions are filled by people with suitable skills and experience, the unanimous shareholder agreement may specifically name certain individuals to serve, for example, as the chief financial officer or chief marketing officer of the company.

The agreement may even require that all of the company's top managers enter into comprehensive employment agreements not only setting out their respective duties, compensation (including bonus entitlement and participation in stock purchase and option plans), and rights on termination, but also their assignment of intellectual property rights and their non-disclosure, non-competition and no "moonlighting" obligations. The need to maintain "key person" insurance for them may also be stipulated.

In order to provide a shareholder with the right to become more involved with the company should the company's financial position deteriorate, the agreement may contain "voting switch" provisions. These provisions give the shareholder the right to elect more directors, even a majority of the company's board, upon the occurrence of certain materially adverse events, such as the failure by the company to meet certain objectives or milestones specified in the agreement or the breach by the company of any covenant in the agreement. Sometimes these provisions even include the right of the shareholder to relieve any of the managers from their management duties upon relatively short notice without cause, but subject to an obligation to pay appropriate severance and to buy back any company shares the managers may hold.

For those companies with just two shareholders having equal or almost equal holdings, the prescribed number of their respective representatives on the board will likely be equal, leaving open the possibility of a deadlocked board on the more contentious issues. Repeated tie votes may result in the company being unable to take necessary action on a number of important matters, much like a partnership with feuding partners being unable to function.

One solution to breaking these possible tie votes is providing in the agreement for a right of the company's chairman to have a second or casting vote on the matter creating the tie. If such a right is included, the parties may insist that the agreement also include a rotation of the chairman position between the two shareholders at certain intervals, since the shareholder with the right to appoint the chairman effectively controls the board.

Each of these rights to appoint board and management representatives must be considered in the context of the company's overall governance and its need for directors and officers who have the skills and experience to properly manage the company's business.

A nominee director or officer still owes a fiduciary duty[11] to the company, not to any particular shareholder. Regardless of being appointed by that shareholder pursuant to a unanimous shareholder agreement, the director or officer may not subordinate the interests of the company while preferring the interests of the nominating shareholder. Individuals who are appointed to key company positions because of their loyalty to their nominating shareholder may soon be unable to reconcile the conflicts between the interests of the company and the interests of the shareholder nominating them.

MAJOR DECISIONS

Most unanimous shareholder agreements impose higher approval thresholds for major decisions. While some agreements simply require a higher than normal percentage for director approval, most agreements require the approval of the shareholders, and often specify a percentage well above a simple majority. It is not uncommon for an agreement to require the approval of three-quarters or four-fifths of the shareholders in order for a major decision to proceed. This need for shareholder approval is an example of the kinds of restrictions on director powers unanimous shareholder agreements contain.

A list of the various company actions that comprise major decisions is often lengthy and is usually attached as a schedule to the agreement. While it sets out a number of actions that can result in an increase in the company's liabilities or a dilution of the current shareholders' percentage interests, many of these actions are qualified or limited by certain exceptions when taken in the normal course of the company's business or if they entail only minor or immaterial liabilities. The list is intended to include any action with the potential to have a material adverse effect on the company or its business.

The list ordinarily includes any changes to the company's articles or by-laws, the issuance of additional shares or securities convertible into shares (other than under an employee share ownership plan or option plan, or as may be required to obtain working capital financing), the redemption or repurchase of company shares, and the payment of any dividends.

Also included are any amalgamation agreement, any asset or share purchase agreement, any partnership or joint venture agreement, and any loan, guarantee or security agreement between the company and any other party. However, borrowing for working capital purposes, whether on a secured or unsecured basis, is generally a permitted exception.

Any proposal or assignment made by the company under applicable insolvency legislation, any attempt to dissolve or liquidate the company, and any pre-payment by the company of any shareholder loans, are other actions likely to appear on the list.

Although the list may stay the same for some time, the percentage approval thresholds may have to change to reflect changes in the percentage holdings of the various shareholders. For example, a current shareholder may not be prepared to invest more money in the company when the other shareholders decline to do so unless the approval thresholds are lowered. The agreement may specify that a lower threshold will apply in the event that the holdings of any shareholder rise above a prescribed percentage. For example, a three-quarters threshold might be reduced to two-thirds when a shareholder ends up with two-thirds of the outstanding shares.

USE OF PROFITS

Shareholders may have different expectations on how and when they will realize a return on their investment in the company. Some may be looking to dividends, while others may be anticipating a large increase in the value of their investment which they will receive when they eventually sell their shares. Some may have a more immediate, short-term view, whereas others, often called "patient capital", may be investing for a longer term.

Since the shareholders are unlikely to have a common view over how often and how much the company should pay them as dividends, the agreement may set out a desired dividend policy for the company to follow when profits permit. The agreement may specify the percentage of the company's earnings, over the amounts needed for operating purposes and required capital expenditures, which is to be distributed to the shareholders as dividends.

Instead of providing guidance for the payment of dividends, the agreement may require that the company's profits first be used to expand the company's operations, or pay down outstanding bank indebtedness, redeem company shares or repay shareholder loans.

BANK FINANCING AND GUARANTEES

Just as the shareholders may have different preferences for the use of the company's profits, they may also have different preferences for how the company raises funds to satisfy its ongoing capital requirements. Some companies have more financing alternatives than others. Those with consistent earnings and substantial assets may be able to choose from a number of sources. Start-up and early stage companies may not be able to secure debt financing and may have to resort to equity capital to fund their growth.

For those companies able to raise money from outside sources, the shareholders may want the agreement to stipulate that the company should first try to obtain new financing from the chartered banks or other financial institutions before calling upon the shareholders for additional funds.

To obtain such financing on reasonable terms, especially in the earlier stages of the company's growth, it may be necessary for one or more of the shareholders to personally guarantee the repayment of all amounts the company may borrow.

The agreement usually addresses this requirement by stipulating that the shareholders provide their personal guarantees to support any bank borrowing so long as their guarantees are limited to a percentage of the amount borrowed which is equal to their percentage shareholding in the company. It may also require the shareholders to indemnify one another if any shareholder becomes liable under her guarantee for more than her percentage interest in the company.

PRE-EMPTIVE RIGHTS

The agreement may also address the company's need to raise equity capital by allowing for voluntary share subscriptions by the current shareholders while providing them with some protection against the dilution of their current percentage holdings. This may be accomplished by giving them pre-emptive rights. As mentioned in the *Additional Shareholder Rights* chapter, these rights apply when the company intends to issue additional shares, which must first be offered to all of the shareholders in proportion to their current holdings.

Notice of the proposed share issuance is to be given by the company to the shareholders, who then have a certain amount of time in which to reply that they want to buy their portion of the offered shares. Each shareholder is usually then given the right to buy more or less than the portion they are offered. If any shareholder subscribes for less than she is entitled to, the balance of the shares she is offered then becomes available for possible issuance to those other shareholders who subscribed for more than the portion to which they were entitled, ordinarily in proportion to their own percentage holdings in the company.

Some agreements may alternatively prevent shareholders from subscribing for more shares than they are offered in the first round. Any unsubscribed shares are to then be re-offered to all participating shareholders based upon their respective percentage holdings until there are no shares left for subscription, or until there are no shareholders left who are willing to subscribe for more shares. If the company has a large number of shareholders, this process of providing notice of each successive offer may be quite time consuming to follow.

The agreement usually provides exemptions from pre-emptive rights for shares issued to employees, officers, directors and consultants pursuant to incentive compensation arrangements, or for shares issued upon conversion of other company securities or in connection with stock dividends or stock splits. Exemptions may also be available for shares issued to commercial lenders and equipment lessors in the ordinary course of business, and shares issued as consideration for the company's acquisition of another business.

MANDATORY SHAREHOLDER FUNDING

In addition to providing for voluntary share subscriptions by the current shareholders through pre-emptive rights, the agreement may impose mandatory subscriptions upon the shareholders as well. The agreement may require the shareholders to invest in additional shares within a certain amount of time after a "capital call" is made upon them. As with pre-emptive rights, capital calls are usually made upon shareholders in proportion to their respective percentage holdings of company shares.

Instead of calling for additional equity investment, the company may require the shareholders to provide additional capital by way of shareholder loans. The shareholders may prefer to advance funds as loans rather than as equity because of the possibility of receiving some security from the company for such loans. Even if their loans are unsecured, they will still rank as creditors in any insolvency or bankruptcy of the company.

While the agreement will likely require them to postpone payment of their loans and subordinate their security in favour of any bank or other financial institution which has provided financing to the company, lending funds to the company may still be preferred over investing in additional equity.

Any decision to include mandatory funding in an agreement should not be made lightly. The relative financial resources of each shareholder need to be considered, especially when such resources could be significantly reduced by the time a call is made. It may be appropriate for capital calls to be made only with the approval of a very high percentage of shareholder votes.

If the agreement does include mandatory funding provisions, it will likely also include a provision specifying what happens if a shareholder is unable or unwilling to satisfy any capital call.

Ordinarily those shareholders who meet their capital calls are given the right to subscribe for the shares or make the loans that a defaulting shareholder was called for. Their exercise of such right in the case of an equity funding call will result in the dilution of the defaulting shareholder's percentage interest. They may also be given an option upon such default to acquire the defaulting shareholder's shares at less than fair market value, resulting in the further dilution or complete transfer of the defaulting shareholder's interest if the option is exercised. In the case of a debt funding call, their additional loans may be set at a higher rate of interest and given a preference to be paid in priority to the company's ordinary shareholder loans.

NEGATIVE COVENANTS

In addition to placing restrictions on the powers of the directors and on the type of business which the company may carry on, the agreement may impose restrictions on the shareholders themselves, particularly on their conduct which may not be in the best interests of the company.

Although the directors are under a statutory duty to act in the best interests of the company, as mentioned above under *Board and Man-*

agement Representation, the shareholders are not. If the shareholders collectively decide that certain contractual duties should be placed upon their fellow shareholders to make up for the absence of certain statutory duties, a unanimous shareholder agreement may also be used for such a purpose.

The agreement may set out various shareholder duties, or "positive covenants", to do certain things. Examples of such covenants appear elsewhere in this book, such as a shareholder's obligation to give notice to the other shareholders of her desire to sell her company shares to an outside party so that they may exercise their rights of first refusal.

But the agreement is just as likely to set out various duties, or "negative covenants", not to do certain things. Examples of these covenants also appear elsewhere in this book, including the companion covenant to the right of first refusal, which prohibits a shareholder from transferring her shares to an outside party.

Three negative covenants that ordinarily appear in the agreement to address possible conflicts of interest between a shareholder and the company are the non-disclosure covenant, the non-solicitation covenant and the non-competition covenant.

Non-disclosure Covenant

A shareholder of a private company is usually required under the agreement not to disclose to anyone outside the company any confidential or proprietary company information, including any intellectual property trade secrets, sales and market data, and any other confidential information relating to the company and its business. This covenant generally applies whether the shareholder continues or ceases to be a shareholder.

The agreement ordinarily provides certain exceptions to this restriction. It does not apply to information known to the public, or information the shareholder knew before becoming a shareholder, or to information the shareholder received from outside parties.

Non-solicitation Covenant

The non-solicitation covenant generally prevents a shareholder from soliciting any employees of the company to become employees of the shareholder, or any customers of the company to become customers of the shareholder, so long as the shareholder remains a shareholder of the company and for a certain period of time afterwards. The survival or continuing enforceability of this covenant generally lasts for a period of between six months and two years after the shareholder disposes of her shares, but longer terms are not unusual.

This provision is usually worded to prohibit only the active solicitation or inducement of company employees or customers by a departing shareholder, and is not intended to cover those employees or customers who approach the shareholder on their own. However, it can lead to a dispute between the company and a departing shareholder who subsequently employs company employees or supplies company customers, since the shareholder's subtle encouragement of the employees and customers is often inferred from the particular circumstances. The shareholder's protest that the employees or customers came on their accord is not always credible.

Non-competition Covenant

In addition to preventing a shareholder from soliciting company employees or customers, the agreement may also try to prevent the shareholder from competing against the company or its affiliates, either directly or indirectly. A non-competition covenant is usually limited to a certain geographical territory or market, and to a certain length of time. It may last as long as a non-solicitation covenant but is sometimes for a slightly shorter period. It represents a much broader restriction than a non-solicitation covenant since a shareholder bound by the latter may continue to participate and invest in the same business as the company.

Its prohibition against both direct and indirect competition ordinarily covers a very broad range of activities. It applies to acting as an employee, officer, director, shareholder, consultant or agent for a competing business, regardless of whether such business is carried on through a partnership, joint venture, trust, other corporation, or even a governmental agency.

Furthermore, the covenant usually prevents the shareholder from lending to, investing in, or otherwise having a financial interest in any business that is the same or substantially similar to the business being carried on by the company or its affiliates. An exception is often made for any investment in publicly traded securities provided such investment represents not more than five per cent of the total securities outstanding of any particular issuer.

Enforcement of Negative Covenants

As monetary damages may not be easily or expeditiously proven before a court or even obtained through the enforcement of a court judgment for a breach of any of these three covenants, the agreement is likely to provide that the company may also ask a court to award an injunction to prevent any continuing breach of them.

Efforts to enforce a non-solicitation or non-competition covenant can face an additional challenge since most courts are reluctant to award a remedy for breach of either covenant if it covers too broad a geographical territory or too long a time period.[12]

The courts have traditionally viewed these two kinds of restrictive covenants as restraints of trade and have needed to be convinced that the covenants are reasonably necessary to protect the company's legitimate proprietary interest before enforcing them. However, customer lists, trade secrets, business connections with customers and goodwill are all legitimate interests worthy of the court's protection.

Often a non-solicitation covenant will be enforced by a court but not a non-competition covenant on the basis that the non-solicitation covenant is all that is necessary to protect a company's interest, provided that it has reasonable territorial and time restrictions.

However, should the company or another shareholder have either a right or obligation to redeem or purchase a shareholder's shares under the agreement, as discussed in greater detail in the previous chapter, there is a greater chance that the non-competition covenant will be enforced by the court, especially if the agreement prescribes the purchase price to be paid for the shares.

Unlike non-competition covenants contained in employment agreements which are seldom enforced, non-competition covenants in share purchase agreements are frequently enforced, due in some part to the equality of bargaining power which ordinarily exists between a purchaser and seller, but not between an employer and employee. Also, a sale of a business often involves a payment for goodwill whereas no similar payment is made to an employee upon leaving employment. Yet in order for the non-competition covenant to be enforceable, it must still contain reasonable territorial and time restrictions.

FAMILY LAW COVENANTS

Because the family laws applicable in many Canadian provinces generally provide a community of property regime which allows for the equalization of family property acquired by spouses during their marriage upon their marriage breakdown, a unanimous shareholder agreement may contain a provision dealing with the implications of such laws upon a shareholder.

Under these laws, a court might order that company shares owned by one spouse be transferred to the other spouse, or that one spouse pay to the other a part of the profits earned by the company. Such orders can lead to a number of undesirable consequences for the company and its shareholders. Control of the company might change, covenants in the company's credit agreements might be breached, and adverse tax effects might result. The provisions in the agreement dealing with board representation and the approval of major decisions may cease to be acceptable to certain shareholders.

Furthermore, such legal proceedings may threaten the confidentiality of sensitive company information, since its financial statements and other records may have to be produced and various details of its business described in a court judgment.

To address some of these potential concerns, the agreement may provide that any shareholder has the right to acquire for a prescribed price the shares of another shareholder who is facing a family law claim for property equalization. This call right, however, has disadvantages for both parties, since it requires the buyer to come up with the purchase funds, which may be difficult to find, and may place an untimely tax liability upon the seller. A court may also be unprepared to accept the prescribed price as the correct value of the shares and wish to undertake its own assessment, thereby again threatening the confidentiality of the company's business information.

A preferred alternative is for the agreement to require the shareholders to have in place separate marriage contracts, with their respective spouses, which exclude their shares from any property equalization and which prevent their spouses from looking to the company to satisfy any equalization payment owing. These marriage contracts would be required immediately from shareholders who are married, and upon any subsequent marriage or remarriage of a shareholder. Any proposed amendment to those contracts that conflicts with the provisions of the unanimous shareholder agreement would have to be approved by all of the shareholders.

Whichever approach is taken, the agreement will still include a provision requiring a shareholder to notify the company and all of the other shareholders if she becomes involved in equalization proceedings.

MISCELLANEOUS MATTERS

In addition to the foregoing items and those items described in the *Additional Shareholder Rights, Buy-Sell Rights* and *Dispute Resolution and Remedies* chapters, the agreement may set out a number of other items that are more procedural in nature or which address the day-to-day operations of the company, whether or not they are also contained in the company's by-laws.

For example, the agreement may specify the company's bankers, lawyers and accountants, its financial year-end, and those persons who are authorized to make bank deposits and sign contracts and cheques.

It may also include any special notice and voting rules for director meetings, the process for preparing and approving operating and capital budgets and the company's business plan, the contents and frequency of financial reports to be distributed to the shareholders, and the delivery of certain files and records for shareholder inspection.

Since the circumstances facing the company or its shareholders are likely to change during the term of the agreement, the procedure for its amendment is usually set out. Unless there are just a few shareholders, requiring the consent of all of the shareholders to any amendment may not be practicable. Normally the consent of a relatively high percentage of shareholders, perhaps 80 per cent, is all that is required to effect an amendment binding upon all of the shareholders.

While the agreement may well have an indefinite term, it may stipulate instead that it is to remain in effect for only a fixed term. The termination of the agreement may occur upon a certain date, upon a certain event taking place or result being achieved, or perhaps in the absence of such event or result by a particular date. Upon termination, the agreement may provide for the company to be liquidated and dissolved, unless the agreement has been terminated to facilitate a public offering of the company's shares.

Shareholder Meetings

As mentioned earlier in this book, it is the shareholders who elect the directors and it is the shareholders who must approve certain company actions before such actions may be carried out. Traditionally such elections and approvals have taken place at a meeting of shareholders, which allowed the shareholders to attend and present their views on the various matters put before the meeting and to raise other issues they felt were relevant to the success of the company.

Many of the shareholder rights already described in the *Individual Statutory Shareholder Rights* and *Collective Statutory Shareholder Rights* chapters may only be exercised at a shareholder meeting, unless it is practicable for a written resolution to be signed by all of the shareholders instead.[1]

For a private company with a relatively large number of shareholders, or whose shareholders are unlikely to act unanimously by way of written resolution, a shareholder meeting will likely be called at least once a year.

This chapter will focus on how a shareholder meeting is called and conducted, but will not address the statutory basis for the rights being exercised at the meeting. Many of the specific rights given to a shareholder under the CBCA that relate to shareholder meetings and which have been described in the *Individual Statutory Shareholder Rights* chapter will not be repeated here. These include the rights to requisition a meeting, solicit proxies, submit proposals, and vote, either in person or by proxy. Neither will the CBCA rights described in the *Collective Statutory Shareholder Rights* chapter be repeated in this chapter.

This chapter will generally look at shareholder meetings called by the directors, although meetings may also be called by requisition of certain shareholders, or by court order as described in the *Dispute Resolution and Remedies* chapter. The calling of a meeting by court order does not necessarily indicate the existence of disputes between the directors and shareholders, but may simply reflect the inability to satisfy the company's quorum requirements, which may be varied or dispensed with at the meeting if the court permits.[2]

ANNUAL MEETINGS

The directors are required to call an annual meeting not later than 18 months after the company comes into existence and then not later than 15 months after the last preceding annual meeting. An annual meeting should be held not later than six months after the company's preceding financial year.[3]

An annual meeting ordinarily covers a number of matters prescribed by the CBCA. It should allow for the consideration of the company's financial statements,[4] appointment of auditors,[5] election of directors,[6] and confirmation of any by-laws enacted during the past year.[7] Though not a statutory requirement, it may also receive the directors' report on the company's operations and confirm all acts of the directors taken in the past year.

SPECIAL MEETINGS

The directors may also call a special meeting for the transaction of any "special" business. Special business is any business other than the consideration of the financial statements and auditor's report, election of directors and reappointment of the incumbent auditor.[8]

PLACE OF MEETINGS

A shareholder meeting is to be held within Canada at the place specified in the company's by-laws, or at the place determined by the directors if not specified in the by-laws. It may, however, be held outside Canada if the company's articles designate such a place or if all of the shareholders agree. Any shareholders attending the meeting outside Canada are deemed to agree unless they are attending to specifically object to the meeting being held.[9]

A meeting does not have to be held "face-to-face" at a common physical location, and may be held by means of an "electronic or other communication facility" unless the company's by-laws otherwise provide.[10]

NOTICE OF MEETING

Notice of the time and place of a shareholder meeting is to be sent not less than 21 days and not more than 60 days[11] before the meeting unless the by-laws or articles of the company provide for a shorter period.[12] The by-laws normally allow the directors to determine the exact time and place of the meeting.

While notice of the meeting is to be sent to every shareholder entitled to vote, every director and the auditor, notice is not required to be sent to shareholders who were not registered on the company's records on the "record date". A record date is the date used for determining the shareholders entitled to receive notice of the meeting, which may be fixed by the directors in advance of giving the notice. If no record date is fixed, it is deemed to be the day before the notice is given. Failure to receive a notice does not deprive a shareholder of the right to vote at the meeting.[13]

The notice must identify the items to be discussed at the meeting. The items normally identified in a notice for an annual meeting include the consideration of the financial statements and auditor's report, election of directors and reappointment of the incumbent auditor. Any other items, to be transacted as special business at a special meeting, are to be identified in the notice in sufficient detail to permit the shareholders to form a reasoned judgment on them, along with the text of any resolution to be submitted to the meeting.[14] Often just one notice of an annual and special meeting combining all of these items will be given.

The company's by-laws are likely to provide that any accidental omission to notify a particular shareholder will not invalidate the business of the meeting. A written waiver of notice of the meeting signed by all of the shareholders or their proxies will normally correct any irregularities in the notice. Usually the company secretary will certify at the meeting the proper mailing of notices and his certificate will be placed in the company's records for the meeting. However, if a meeting is held without proper notice and if even just one shareholder does not sign a proxy or waiver or otherwise consent to the business conducted, the business may be declared invalid.[15]

ADJOURNMENT OF MEETING

The by-laws are also likely to provide that the chair, upon convening the meeting, with the consent of the meeting and subject to any conditions as the meeting may decide, may adjourn the meeting from time to time and place to place.

If the meeting is adjourned for fewer than 30 days, there is no need to give a further notice of the adjourned meeting unless the by-laws so require. If it is adjourned by one or more adjournments totaling 30 days or more, then notice of the adjourned meeting must be given as if an original meeting.[16]

PREPARATION FOR A MEETING

In preparing for a shareholder meeting, especially an annual meeting which will be dealing with special business, the chair's agenda is drafted well in advance of the meeting. The agenda will often attempt to include additional items which may arise at the meeting, scheduling the essential items for early in the meeting and deferring more contentious items until later.

The number of contentious items expected to be discussed, and the number of shareholders entitled to attend and vote, will influence the extent of the preparation undertaken. Ballots may have to be produced in anticipation that a poll will be called for instead of a show of hands on certain matters, and independent scrutineers may have to be appointed to oversee the voting process. It may be expedient for routine motions to be read by "movers" and "seconders" who have been selected beforehand. The chair will usually be well coached to answer a variety of questions which may asked by the shareholders.

The chair is most likely to be the officer designated in the by-laws to chair the meeting, often the company's president. If no chair has been designated, the shareholders present may select one of their number to chair the meeting.

CONDUCT OF THE MEETING

Upon calling the meeting to order, the chair will attempt to ascertain whether a quorum is present. If the holders of a majority of the shares entitled to vote at the meeting are present in person or represented by proxy, there will be a sufficient quorum to proceed regardless of the number of persons actually present, unless the by-laws stipulate otherwise.[17] It may be necessary to involve scrutineers to make this determination.

Once quorum has been established, the chair will then declare that the meeting may proceed. Even if quorum is lost at any time throughout the meeting, the meeting may continue on unless the by-laws provide to the contrary. If a quorum cannot be established at the outset, the meeting may be adjourned by the shareholders present but they may not transact any other business.[18]

The meeting then commences with a reading of the notice of the meeting and a tabling of the secretary's certificate that the notice, financial statements and other documents have been properly sent as required. The minutes of the previous shareholder meeting may then be read, or more likely, a motion will be requested for the minutes to be taken as read. The minutes may then be signed, or corrected and then signed if an amendment is requested.

Each item set out in the meeting agenda will then by dealt with by the chair requesting that a motion in respect of the item be made, seconded, and then submitted to the shareholders for their discussion, possible amendment and vote. The chair normally decides upon any questions regarding the meeting's procedures but must act fairly to all the shareholders present and comply with any rules of procedure prescribed in the company's by-laws. However, the chair must ensure that the business identified in the notice of the meeting is completed, and may therefore be required to cut short those speakers wandering off topic.

If an amendment to any motion is proposed, it should only vary the original motion in some detail. The chair should refuse to allow an amendment to be proposed if it introduces an essentially new item or is completely negative to the original motion, and call for a new motion instead. If the chair allows an amendment to be proposed, the amendment should be voted on first. If it loses, the original motion should then be put to the meeting. If the amendment wins, it should be included in the original motion and voted on again as a motion that supersedes the original motion. If the amended motion loses, the original motion is not revived.

The chair may end the discussion on any item and put that item to a vote if the meeting approves a motion to do so. A vote is ordinarily taken by a show of hands unless a ballot is demanded by a shareholder or proxyholder. However, where a resolution needs to be passed by a certain percentage of the shares held or votes cast, such as a special resolution which requires a majority of not less than two-thirds of the votes cast a ballot should be taken. If scrutineers have been appointed, they will report the results of any ballot to the chair who will, in turn, announce the results to the meeting and declare whether or not the resolution has been adopted by the required majority. Their written report on the actual vote is ordinarily presented after the meeting and attached to the minutes of the meeting.

After completion of all of the items on the agenda, the chair usually asks the meeting if there is any other business. If new business is raised at that time, the chair has to decide if such business falls within the purpose for which the meeting was called before allowing it to be considered by the meeting. If no new business is raised, the chair may then adjourn the meeting with its consent.

Director Duties

It has already been stated that the directors have the statutory power and duty to manage, or supervise the management of, the company's business and affairs. Even though this general duty is subject to the rights granted to the shareholders under the CBCA and subject to a number of additional rights the shareholders may acquire, the directors are still required to carry out a number of specific duties.

This chapter will describe some of these duties. As well as examining the overriding fiduciary duty and duty of care imposed upon the directors, it will set out a number of other duties the directors are supposed to perform under the CBCA when managing the company's business. Some of the liabilities the directors may face, the means of avoiding such liabilities, and their rights to be indemnified by the company, in carrying out their duties will also be discussed.

However, this chapter will not describe the numerous duties imposed upon directors under other federal statutes as well as under the statutes of the various provinces in which the company may be operating. Numbering possibly in the hundreds if the company operates across Canada, these statutes affect most corporate functions and cover many areas, including taxation, competition, securities, employment insurance, health and safety, pensions, the environment, and many more.

While the directors are given the overall power to manage the company, they don't have to exercise all of this power together. They may delegate many of their powers to committees of directors or to a managing director.[1] Even their borrowing power can be delegated to a director or committee of directors, or to an officer.[2] However, a director may not act by a proxy or substitute.

The right to delegate is often exercised by relatively large boards, which have difficulty convening frequent board meetings on short notice.

Since committees have fewer members than the full board, they are often used to deal with urgent matters. As particular committees are usually comprised of directors with skills and interest in specific areas, they are also used to address matters within those areas.

However, not all matters may be delegated by the board to a committee or managing director. For example, filling a vacancy among the directors or in the office of auditor, issuing debt securities and shares, declaring dividends, acquiring and redeeming shares, paying commissions on the purchase of shares, approving financial statements and passing by-laws require the authority of the full board.[3] These particular matters are left to the full board since it may incur liability if they are improperly handled.

While relatively few private companies have more than just one or two committees of directors, if they have any committees at all, there is no shortage of committees that may be set up if the practices of some public companies are to be followed. The following chapter on *Governance* explores this topic in greater detail.

An executive committee is the most likely to be established. It is ordinarily delegated all of the powers the full board has to conduct the on-going business of the company, except for those matters referred to above which cannot be delegated.

An audit committee is also frequently appointed, comprised of directors with certain financial expertise, although its mandate often goes beyond strict financial matters. It may be expected to monitor the effectiveness of internal controls, risk management guidelines and management information systems. Audit committees required under the CBCA for distributing corporations must review the company's financial statements before being submitted to the board for approval, and they must have a majority of members who are not officers or employees.[4]

In addition to these two committees, the board may establish a compensation committee to set appropriate levels of management compensation and perhaps handle other matters relating to human resources, such as employee benefit plans. This committee is usually comprised of non-management directors. The board may also establish a nominating committee for the purpose of identifying possible directors, and depending upon the nature of the company's business, an environmental committee.

Some committees are established to serve on a temporary basis in order to investigate and consider a particular issue, and then either report to the board or take its own actions to resolve the issue. Sometimes these special committees appoint their own counsel and experts, whose advice they may then rely upon in the exercise of their own duty of care. Special committees are generally regarded as the preferred way to solve problems that the board, attempting to deal with them on its own, might address inappropriately and thereby incur legal liability.

If the board establishes a committee without any power to act on the board's behalf but to instead report back and recommend to the board on certain matters, such a committee need not be comprised of only directors.

Whether a particular matter is addressed by the full board or by a committee, any director participating in the discussions and ultimate resolution made on such matters must be aware of her broad fiduciary duty and duty of care.

FIDUCIARY DUTY

The directors are required to act honestly and in good faith with a view to the best interests of the company when exercising their powers and discharging their duties.[5] Because this duty reflects the fiduciary relationship between each director and the company, the director is often described as a trustee of the company. However, the description is not entirely accurate, since company directors make decisions entailing a variety of business risks, whereas trustees are essentially engaged in the preservation of property.

This fiduciary duty is owed to the company and not to any particular group of stakeholders, such as the shareholders. Often the interests of the shareholders and other stakeholders are the same as the interests of the company, but if they conflict, the directors' duty is clearly to the company. The duty is not confined to short-term profit or share value, but to the company's long-term interests, assuming it remains a going concern. In determining how to proceed on any particular matter, the directors may ordinarily rely upon their own business judgment, in accordance with the business judgment rule described below.[6]

In order to act honestly and in good faith with regard to the company, the directors must respect the trust and confidence given to them to manage the company's assets. They must avoid conflicts of interest with the company. They must avoid abusing their director position to gain personal benefit. They must keep confidential the information they acquire because of their position.[7]

Disclosing Conflicts of Interest

Because the directors are in a fiduciary relationship with the company, they must not profit from any transactions involving the company without the knowledge and consent of the company. They must not be in a position where their personal interests will conflict with their duties as a director. However, they may deal with the company and keep any profit resulting from the transaction if they have made full disclosure to the company and the company has consented to it.

The CBCA requires a director to disclose in writing, or have recorded in the minutes of a meeting of directors, the nature and extent of any interest she may have in a material contract or transaction with the company, whether it is made or proposed. The director personally may be a party, or a director or officer of a party, or have a material interest in a party, to the contract or transaction.[8] There are no specific rules regarding the amount of detail the director should disclose but the other directors should be sufficiently informed about the director's interest before they make a decision.

There are, however, specific rules for the timing of the director's disclosure.[9] Disclosure must be made at the meeting at which the proposed contract is first considered. If the director was not then interested, or becomes interested after the contract is made, disclosure must be made at the first meeting after she becomes interested. If an individual who is interested in a contract later becomes a director, disclosure must be made at the first meeting after she becomes a director.

If a material contract or transaction is one that would not ordinarily be presented to the board for approval, the director must still disclose her interest in it by notifying the board in writing or requesting that her interest be recorded in the minutes of the meetings of directors.[10]

A director having an interest in a material contract or transaction may not vote on it unless it relates primarily to her remuneration, or is for indemnity or insurance.[11]

In light of these requirements, many directors provide their board with a general declaration of interest, which identifies all the organizations of which they are a director or officer, or in which they have a material interest. This declaration is usually provided when the director is first appointed and then regularly updated, often annually.

A contract or transaction requiring disclosure does not become invalid, and the director does not have to account for any profit made from it, just because the director had an interest in it, so long as three conditions are met. First, the director had to disclose her interest as required. Second, the other directors had to approve the contract or transaction. And third, the contract or transaction had to be reasonable and fair to the company at the time it was approved.[12]

This third condition can be difficult to satisfy, especially if the director's interest is attacked years later in a court proceeding and the board's approval is viewed in the light of subsequent events. Even if the contract or transaction has been approved by the shareholders by way of a special resolution, it may still not be saved if the court finds it was not reasonable and fair to the company when it was approved.[13]

Avoiding Misuse of Corporate Opportunity

Related to their duty to disclose their potential conflicts of interest and also arising out of their fiduciary relationship with the company, the directors should not take for themselves or divert to a related party a maturing business opportunity the company is actively pursuing. The opportunity rightfully belongs to the company.[14]

Resigning from the board before taking up such an opportunity does not get around this prohibition if the resignation was prompted by the desire to take advantage of the opportunity. Even if the company could not have made a profit if it pursued the opportunity itself, the directors taking it up are still not relieved of their fiduciary obligations to the company. Only when the opportunity is a fresh initiative that is later acquired by the directors will they be permitted to pursue it.

Unless a director makes sufficient disclosure to the company and secures its consent before proceeding to take up the opportunity, she may well be liable to account to the company for her profits.

DUTY OF CARE

The directors are required to exercise the care, diligence and skill that a reasonably prudent person would exercise in comparable circumstances when exercising their powers and discharging their duties.[15] While boards are composed of directors with a variety of skills, no one director is expected to be skilled in all areas of the company's business.

However, in those areas where a director is not skilled, the director is expected to make diligent inquiries and perhaps seek outside advice. A director can comply with this duty of care by relying in good faith upon financial statements presented by the company's officers or contained in an auditor's report, or upon reports from professional advisers such as accountants, lawyers, valuation experts or engineers.[16]

Unlike the fiduciary duty described above, which is owed solely to the company, this duty of care can be owed by the directors to the company's various stakeholders.[17] These may include the shareholders, employees, creditors, consumers, governments and the environment.

Because of the vast number of laws governing a company's conduct, as well as imposing responsibility upon the directors for seeing that such laws are complied with, the directors are often required to prove in any legal proceedings brought against them or the company under such laws that they have exercised care, diligence and skill by developing policies and procedures to ensure compliance with these laws by company personnel. Some form of reporting system should be put into place allowing the directors to monitor the ongoing effectiveness of their policies.

Business Judgment Rule

The possible liability faced by directors under their duty of care is influenced by the "business judgment rule" being applied by the courts. Under this rule, the courts have been deferential to board decisions so long as the directors have acted reasonably and fairly.[18]

Provided the directors have made a reasonable decision, though not necessarily a perfect decision, a court will not substitute its opinion for that of the board even though subsequent events have cast doubt on the board's determination. The board need only have selected from a number of reasonable alternatives.

Board decisions, in other words, will not be subject to microscopic examination, since the courts have generally been reluctant to interfere with the board's function to manage. They have generally recognized that a board decision must often be made under considerable time pressure when detailed information may not be available. The courts have also recognized that they may be ill-suited to make certain business decisions and shouldn't second-guess the application of the board's particular expertise.

However, the courts are capable of determining whether an appropriate degree of diligence has been exercised by a board. If a court finds the manner in which the board arrived at a decision to be lacking, the business judgment rule cannot be used to save the decision. If the board followed a flawed process in making a decision, perhaps by acting too quickly without due consideration of other alternatives, a board decision may be overturned.[19]

OTHER DIRECTOR DUTIES

Acquisition and Redemption of Shares

The directors may authorize the acquisition and redemption of the company's shares provided that the company is able to satisfy the statutory solvency tests.[20] If the company fails to meet these tests, the directors will be jointly and severally liable to restore to the company the funds that were improperly paid out.[21] However, the directors may then ask a court to compel any shareholder receiving an improper amount to pay such amount to the directors.[22]

Because solvency tests must be satisfied by the company in order for the directors to authorize share purchases and redemptions, as well as declare dividends as mentioned below, they are expected to have independent appraisals of the realizable value of the company's assets made available to them. Compliance with these tests cannot be ensured by referring to the company's financial statements alone, since the balance sheet may reflect only the historical cost of the assets, not their current realizable value.

Ordinarily the company's shares are cancelled upon acquisition, since the company is generally prohibited from holding its own share; although there are a few limited exceptions. Even if the company is allowed to hold its own shares, such shares may not be voted unless held by the company as a legal representative for another party.[23]

Approval of Financial Statements

The company is required to send financial statements to each shareholder before the annual meeting unless the shareholder doesn't want to receive them.[24] Before the statements are mailed, they must be approved by the directors. Approval is usually evidenced by the signature of two authorized directors.

Appointment of Officers

Officers may be appointed by the directors.[25] Often the directors appoint officers for the ensuing year at a meeting immediately following the annual shareholder meeting at which the directors are elected. However, apart from a managing director, there is no provision in the CBCA for the appointment of other officers, including a president or secretary.

Unless the articles, by-laws or unanimous shareholder agreement otherwise provide, the appointment of officers by the board is undertaken pursuant to its general power to manage the company's business and affairs. Still, any officers appointed are subject to the same fiduciary duty and duty of care as apply to the directors, as discussed above.[26]

Authorizing Payment of Commissions

The directors may authorize the company to pay a reasonable commission to anyone who procures buyers for the company's shares.[27] However, if the commissions are excessive, the directors will be jointly and severally liable to reimburse the company for the commissions that were improperly paid out. [28]

Borrowing

Without the authorization of the shareholders, but subject to the articles, by-laws or unanimous shareholder agreement, the directors may borrow money on the credit of the company, issue or pledge debt obligations of the company, give company guarantees, and mortgage or pledge the company's property to secure any company obligations.[29]

Compliance with CBCA and Company Charter

The directors are required to comply with the CBCA and its regulations, the company's articles and by-laws, and any unanimous shareholder agreement. No provision in the articles or by-laws, or in any resolution or contract, may relieve a director of the duty to act in accordance with the CBCA and its regulations, nor relieve the director of liability for breach of either.[30]

An exception to this prohibition is made for unanimous shareholder agreements to the extent they transfer any duties from the directors to the shareholders.

Declaration of Dividends

The directors may declare dividends provided that the company can meet the statutory solvency test.[31] Even though sufficient profits exist to allow for the payment of dividends, a shareholder is not entitled to require the company to pay dividends. Although the company's general by-law is likely to provide that the directors may declare and pay dividends from time to time out of funds available for that purpose, the declaration of dividends is one of the board functions that may not be delegated to a committee of directors or to a managing director.

Although dividends were traditionally payable only out of profits, they may be distributed out of other sources by the directors at their discretion so long as the solvency test can be met. For example, dividends may be paid even if the company has sustained a temporary loss, in order to satisfy the shareholders' long-standing expectations for regular dividends. They may also be paid out of the capital appreciation of company assets, whether such appreciation has resulted in realized gains or not, particularly when depreciation expenses have been taken for assets, which effectively did not depreciate.

Furthermore, dividends may be paid out of surpluses even if the surpluses are invested in inventory or receivables and are not represented by cash balances. Although the directors may be reluctant to borrow in order to pay cash dividends, they may do so if the company meets the solvency test.

Directors who authorize payment of a dividend when the company fails to meet this test will be jointly and severally liable to restore to the company the funds that were improperly paid out.[32] However, the directors may then ask a court to compel any shareholder receiving an improper dividend to pay the amount of the dividend to the directors.[33] But the directors will not be liable if they exercised due diligence when authorizing the payment, perhaps by relying upon the company's audited financial statements.[34]

Subject to the dividend rights that attach to a particular class of shares, as described in the *Additional Shareholder Rights* chapter, the directors may be given in the company's articles the discretion to declare different dividends on different classes of shares. For a private company with just a few shareholders, especially for a family-owed company whose shareholders are related to each other, the directors may then engage in "income splitting" by declaring the largest dividend on the class of shares held by the family member with the lowest income and marginal tax rate.[35]

In addition to declaring cash dividends, the directors may authorize payment of dividends in property or fully paid shares, subject to any restrictions in the company's articles or unanimous shareholder agreement. If the dividend is to be paid in property, the company must be able to satisfy the solvency test.[36]

If the dividend is to be paid in company shares, the declared amount of the dividend in money is to be added to the stated capital account for the shares. These stock dividends allow the company to distribute some of its surplus to the shareholders without using cash needed for company operations. Stock dividends may be issued as shares of the same class or as shares of another class.

When declaring dividends, the directors must be aware of any other restrictions on dividends that may be contained in the company's financing agreements. The company may have entered into debentures, mortgages, loan agreements or trust deeds, which contain various covenants limiting the amount and frequency of dividends that may be paid, or prohibiting the payment of any dividends without the consent of the financing party unless they are mandatory under the terms of the shares.

Filling Director and Auditor Vacancies

The directors may fill a vacancy among the directors or in the office of auditor, or appoint additional directors.[37]

Fixing Remuneration

The directors may fix the remuneration of the directors, officers and employees of the company, subject to the articles, the by-laws or any unanimous shareholder agreement.[38]

Issuance of Shares

Shares of the company may be issued at such times, to such persons, and for such consideration as the directors may determine, even though such issuance may be opposed by certain shareholders. However, shares may not be issued until the consideration is paid in money, or in property or past services that are not less in value than the fair equivalent of the money the company would have received if the shares had been issued for money. The directors therefore have to determine the value of the property or past services received. Acceptable consideration does not include a promissory note or other promise to pay.[39]

If the directors issue shares for property worth less than the fair equivalent of money the company would have received, they will be jointly and severally liable to the company to make good the deficiency.[40] One exception to this prohibition is the issuance of stock dividends, as discussed above.

Passing By-laws

The directors may pass by-laws regulating the business and affairs of the company unless the articles, by-laws or a unanimous shareholder agreement provide otherwise. Any by-laws made by the directors are subject to the approval of the shareholders at the next shareholder meeting, at which time the by-laws may be confirmed, amended or repealed.[41]

DIRECTOR INDEMNIFICATION AND INSURANCE

The company is specifically permitted under the CBCA to indemnify a director against all costs, charges and expenses, including any amount paid to settle an action or satisfy a judgment, reasonably incurred by the director in respect of any civil, criminal, administrative, investigative or other proceeding in which the director was involved because of her association with the company.[42] The company may even advance funds to the director for her costs, charges and expenses related to such proceedings.[43] The company's by-laws may well require director indemnification consistent with these CBCA provisions.

The main purpose of indemnification is to provide assurance to those willing to serve as directors that they will be compensated by the company for any adverse consequences arising from their well-intentioned commercial decisions made on behalf of the company. However, while attempting to encourage director entrepreneurism, the CBCA discourages director misconduct by prohibiting corporate indemnification in certain circumstances.

A director may not be indemnified, and may have to repay any funds advanced to her, unless she acted honestly and in good faith with a view to the best interests of the company. In the case of criminal or administrative proceedings enforced by a monetary penalty, she must also have had reasonable grounds for believing her conduct was lawful. If she meets these conditions, and is not judged by a court or other authority to have been at fault, she is entitled to be indemnified whether the company wishes to indemnify her or not.[44]

Determining whether a director is able to meet these good faith and lawful conduct requirements in order to qualify for indemnification can be difficult. A company may attempt to deny indemnification if the director was engaged in opportunistic or self-seeking behaviour, or if her conduct was inexplicable, perhaps reckless, giving rise to the inference that she was acting in bad faith.[45] It may also deny indemnification if the director's belief that her conduct was lawful was unreasonable given that such belief would be obviously erroneous to the "most untrained observer".[46]

The company is allowed to purchase and maintain insurance for the benefit of the director in her capacity as a director.[47] Such insurance is often a director's only means of recovery if the company becomes insolvent and is unable to make any indemnity payments. Claims against directors generally increase when a company is insolvent. Insurance coverage, however, is not necessarily available to every company on an affordable basis, and usually excludes certain areas of significant director exposure, including environmental liability.

Those directors who are serving on the company's board as nominees of a larger shareholder may also be protected by an indemnity agreement provided to them by that shareholder when they begin their term as a director.

Governance

In addition to the duties and restrictions that may be placed on the directors by way of the company's articles, by-laws, share conditions or unanimous shareholder agreement, the power of the directors to manage may also be affected by the governance procedures the company may adopt.

Some shareholders may be in a position to insist that certain governance procedures be implemented as a condition of making their investment in the company. Other shareholders may be able to persuade the directors to adopt such procedures simply because it's good business to do so.

Public companies are expected to voluntarily comply with recommended governance standards and are required to publicly disclose what governance structures they do have in place.[1] Private companies are not. But while many private companies may be unwilling or unable to conform to these higher standards, if they are even aware such standards exist, some may be better off if they try to conform as best they can. The failure to respect good governance may place the company at a competitive disadvantage in the marketplace, not only in selling its products and services but also in obtaining financing from outside sources.

Many private companies, especially those with just a few shareholders, lack effective governance structures. Their boards are often in place only to "rubber stamp" those decisions of management that need to have board approval to satisfy a request from a banker, supplier or other third party, or to meet a technical legislative requirement. And their boards are often comprised of only the major shareholder and his family members. Yet many of these private companies like it this way. After all, many feel the absence of governance is one of the benefits of being private, with little bureaucracy to slow things down.

BENEFITS OF GOOD GOVERNANCE

However, a board or board committee with a few members who are independent of the major shareholder and management can serve as more than just a comforting watchdog for the other shareholders on the prowl for conflicts of interest and digging up personal expenses being disguised as business expenses.

In addition to keeping management "honest" by overseeing transactions that might benefit the major shareholder but not the company, such a board or committee can also serve as a vehicle for arriving at better informed decisions. The senior executive of a private company can often benefit from the objective review and advice of others who are familiar with the company though separate from it. Setting company strategy and planning for growth, as well as realistically assessing ongoing performance, can often be done more effectively with the help of outsiders having broader perspectives.

But not just better informed decisions can be made. Tough decisions can be made as well.

A board comprised of just the major shareholder and his family members may be less inclined to initiate changes that may threaten their own personal interests, even though such changes may be badly needed by the company in order to keep up with the competition. Removing unqualified family members from executive positions, putting in place a business succession plan, cutting long-standing ties with an underperforming supplier or loyal but non-paying customer, dropping an unprofitable product which was invented by the major shareholder, or taking away various perquisites like expensive cars and clubs, are more likely to be suggested by a board or committee consisting of a few outsiders.

In addition to enabling tough as well as better informed decisions to be made, more rigorous governance standards are supposed to provide greater transparency of the process followed in arriving at such decisions. They are also supposed to facilitate accountability of those making the decisions. It's not only the shareholders, but also the employees, creditors and other stakeholders of the company, who take some comfort in knowing who makes the decisions and how the decisions are made.

RESISTANCE TO GOOD GOVERNANCE

Despite the benefits that may be gained through the implementation of better governance structures, some private companies take the view that such structures just aren't for them. Many feel they are just too small, lacking the breadth of resources and operations which justify the maintenance of such structures. If they have only a few shareholders, all of whom are actively involved in management, they may feel there is no need for independent watchdogs, and that their decision-making process works just fine, with no need for a fix. They may feel that they are so "closely held" that they already have as much transparency and accountability as they want or need.

If they have never appointed an outside accounting firm to perform an audit in connection with their annual financial statements, how can they be convinced of the merits of appointing outside directors to serve on board committees? Why should they adopt a shareholder communication policy and feedback structure for just a few people? Why should they incur the time and expense in setting up and maintaining audit, nominating and compensation committees which may well turn out to be too unwieldy to deal quickly with fleeting opportunities?

Some of the benefits gained from governance structures recommended for public companies can be gained in the private company context by way of contract, without putting such structures into place. Subscription agreements and shareholder agreements can provide private company shareholders with ready access to information, and with rights to review and veto proposed transactions if they so choose, whether or not they sit on the company's board or on a board committee, and whether or not the board or its committees are comprised only of insiders. The shareholders of public companies don't ordinarily enjoy such contractual rights.

PRESSURES TO IMPLEMENT GOOD GOVERNANCE

The reluctance of a private company to implement more comprehensive governance structures may be understandable so long as it is financed by supportive family and friends. It may have to change its position, however, when it attempts to raise funds from other sources. Venture capitalists and other professional investors are starting to insist that the private companies they invest in adopt many of the governance practices now followed by public companies.

Not only do these investors want increased governance to ensure transparency, accountability and good decision making in order to protect their investment, they also want increased governance to protect their own nominees on the board who are under a director's duty to exercise care, diligence and skill. They also have to account to their own corporate and institutional shareholders, many of whom are under strict governance standards themselves. These standards often have to be observed by the professional investors and by the companies they invest in.

Since an initial public offering of the company, or a sale of the company to a third party, can provide an exit from their investment, professional investors often insist that increased governance be put into place when the company is private in order to make it easier for the company to either go public or be acquired by a public company.

RECOMMENDED GOVERNANCE STRUCTURES AND PRACTICES

Recommending one generic package of governance standards and practices to be adopted by each and every private company would be misguided. There are just too many variations of private company ownership. Some private companies have just one shareholder, but that shareholder may be an individual with little business expertise, or a large public corporation with operations around the world. While other private companies have a number of shareholders, the shareholders may all be full-time officers of the company, or they may have had nothing to do with the company since they invested in it years before. Some private companies have one controlling shareholder, others don't.

When a private company is prepared to put more comprehensive governance structures into place, either at its own instigation or upon the request of a professional investor as a condition to funding, it has a number of alternatives to consider. Most of the alternatives are conveniently included in the corporate governance guidelines recommended by the securities regulators for Canadian public companies. Some of the guidelines are inappropriate for certain kinds of private companies. Actually, some are even inappropriate for certain kinds of public companies.[2]

The guidelines recommended for public companies generally address the process a company should follow in selecting, orienting, compensating and assessing directors, and in promoting ethical business conduct, but don't address the specific tasks which should be assigned to the board or the decisions requiring the board's prior approval. Although they recommend that the board assume responsibility for strategic planning, risk management, management succession planning, and corporate governance, the guidelines don't prescribe what goes on a board's agenda. They do, however, recommend the establishment of nominating and compensation committees of the board, in addition to the audit committee which is required for public companies by law.

Although "best" governance structures and practices will continue to evolve for all companies, both public and private, private companies evaluating their current governance structures have to start somewhere. Perhaps they should start by addressing what are often regarded as the fundamentals of corporate governance. These fundamentals include independent directors, nominating and compensation committees as well as an audit committee (assuming outside auditors are already engaged), a code of business conduct, director orientation and continuing education programs, and the regular assessment of director performance. These recommended structures and practices are described in more detail below.

The Board and Independent Directors

The board should have a majority of independent directors, and the chair of the board should be an independent director. If it's not appropriate for the chair to be independent, an independent director should be appointed to act as "lead director" to ensure that essential tasks make it onto the board's agenda. The independent directors should hold regularly scheduled meetings which members of management do not attend.

In order to be independent, a director must not have a relationship with the company, or with a subsidiary or parent of the company, which would be expected to interfere with the director's independent judgment.

Audit Committee

An audit committee should be established by the board, preferably consisting of only independent directors who have a good grasp of financial statements. The audit committee should recommend to the board the external auditors to be nominated for appointment by the shareholders, and the compensation to be paid to the auditors. It should oversee the work of the external auditors and attempt to resolve any disagreements between the auditors and management over financial reporting.

The audit committee should also pre-approve all non-audit services to be provided to the company by the external auditors, and review the company's financial statements before being released generally to the shareholders or other stakeholders. It should have authority to communicate directly with both the company's internal and external auditors.

Nominating Committee

The board should create a nominating committee, preferably with only independent directors, to assist the board in nominating or appointing individuals to serve as board members or committee members.

The nominating committee should help the board identify what competencies and skills the board, as a whole, should possess, and assess what competencies and skills each existing director possesses. The nominating committee should determine what competencies and skills each new nominee should bring to the board, and should recommend individuals with such competencies and skills to be nominated as new directors at the next annual meeting of shareholders.

Compensation Committee

A compensation committee, preferably with only independent directors, should be set up by the board to review and approve the company's objectives which are relevant to the Chief Executive Officer's compensation, to evaluate the CEO's performance in light of the objectives, and to determine the CEO's compensation level based on the evaluation. The compensation committee should also make recommendations to the board regarding non-CEO officer and director compensation, incentive-compensation plans and equity-based plans.

Code of Business Conduct and Ethics

A written code of business conduct and ethics should be adopted by the board which applies to all of the company's directors, officers and employees. Designed to promote integrity and deter wrongdoing, it should address conflicts of interest, including transactions and agreements in which a director or executive officer has a material interest.

The code should prescribe the proper use and protection of corporate assets and opportunities, confidentiality of company information, compliance with laws and regulations, and reporting of any illegal or unethical behavior. It should also require that all of the company's security holders, customers, suppliers, competitors and employees are dealt with fairly.

The board should be responsible for monitoring compliance with the code, and only the board or a board committee should be able to permit non-compliance by an individual in particular circumstances.

Director Orientation and Continuing Education

All new directors should receive a comprehensive orientation so that they fully understand the role of the board and its committees, the contribution they are individually expected to make, and the nature and operation of the company's business. All directors should be provided with continuing education opportunities, not only to maintain or enhance their skills and abilities as directors, but also to ensure they remain current in their knowledge and understanding of the company's business.

Regular Board Assessments

The board, its committees and each individual director should be regularly assessed regarding their respective effectiveness and contribution to the company. The assessment of each individual director should be based upon the role that the director was expected to play on the board as well as upon the competencies and skills the director was expected to bring.

IMPLEMENTING GOOD GOVERNANCE

Once a private company has compared its current governance structures and practices with the above fundamentals and concludes a few things are missing, it then faces the decision of what to change and what to leave as is. For the company with professional investors as shareholders, it probably won't have much choice unless it is a start-up or early stage company. It is likely to be asked to put the fundamentals into place if it hasn't already done so, although there may be considerable overlap in the membership of its committees and the members themselves may not be fully independent.

For those private companies that have a choice, the decision of what's in and what's out is not easily made. Being convinced of the benefits of good governance is one thing, but having the time and resources to implement and maintain it is another.

Perhaps all that can be easily decided is that the fundamentals will not be put into place all at once. They are more likely to be phased in over time. While recruiting individuals who are truly independent to serve as directors is not an easy task, having at least one independent director is a good step to take. Having a code of business conduct is another. Nominating and compensation committees with only independent directors, or director performance reviews and continuing education, may follow later.

Dispute Resolution and Remedies

Although private company shareholders may have the right to oversee the directors' management of the company by way of votes at shareholder meetings, they do not manage the company unless a unanimous shareholder agreement provides otherwise. Consequently their desires to be involved in company decision-making are often frustrated and their rights to challenge or overturn company actions are quite limited.

But they are not necessarily forced to rely upon shareholder meetings as their only forum for the scrutiny and criticism of the company. They may be able to take their disputes with management to the courts for adjudication in certain circumstances. Alternatively, they may have recourse to mediation and arbitration if they are party to a shareholder agreement that provides them with dispute resolution procedures.

As described earlier in this book, the CBCA provides that the directors, not the shareholders, are responsible for the company's management. In performing this role, the directors are under a fiduciary duty to act honestly and in good faith with a view to the best interests of the company. They are also under a duty of care to exercise the care, diligence and skill that a reasonably prudent person would exercise in comparable circumstances.[1]

Their fiduciary duty is owed to the company. In carrying out their fiduciary duty, the directors are supposed to look at the interests of the company's shareholders, as well as the interests of the employees, creditors, consumers, governments and the environment, when considering what is in the best interests of the company.[2] But their fiduciary duty is still to the company only, leaving open the possibility that they may disregard the interests of some of the shareholders.

However, a number of special remedies are available to protect shareholder interests. Traditionally only the beneficiary of a fiduciary duty was able to enforce it. If the company was the beneficiary, the directors managing the company were unlikely to sue themselves for breach of their own fiduciary duty. These special remedies get around that problem and provide the shareholders with recourse.

One of the remedies is the "derivative action", which allows shareholders to enforce the directors' duty to the company when the directors themselves are unwilling to do so. Shareholders are also able to bring a civil action for breach of the directors' duty of care, as well as an "oppression action" to seek compensation for the oppressive acts of the company or the directors. They may also apply to the courts for assistance in ordering that certain corporate action be taken.

Furthermore, court approval is required if the company intends to implement certain fundamental changes which affect the rights of shareholders. The shareholders are thereby able to argue before the court against any change proposed.

Some of these shareholder remedies and possible recourse to the courts are discussed in greater detail in this chapter. The use of mediation and arbitration, often prescribed in unanimous shareholder agreements as an alternative to involving the courts in resolving disputes between the shareholders themselves, is described first in this chapter.

Many of the shareholder rights referred to in this book are based not upon statute law but upon contract law, as described in the *Additional Shareholder Rights*, *Buy-Sell Rights*, and *Unanimous Shareholder Agreements* chapters. The remedies ordinarily associated with breach of contract, namely claims for damages or for specific performance of a contract, will not be discussed in this chapter.

MEDIATION AND ARBITRATION

Although alternative dispute resolution or "ADR" clauses in unanimous shareholder agreements come in many different forms, those reflecting a combination of mediation and arbitration are becoming more commonplace, with the disputing shareholders required to first try mediation. Only if their efforts at mediation fail may they then proceed to arbitration to resolve their disagreement, rather than to litigation. Unlike litigation which exposes a dispute to public scrutiny by way of court filings and proceedings, mediation and arbitration can be conducted in private.

Because the resolution of a dispute by mediation requires the consent of the parties to it, mediation alone as an ADR provision may not be very effective.

Many mediation clauses address how the mediator is to be appointed, which is often by mutual agreement. Failing such agreement, the clause may require that the mediator is to be appointed by a specific organization.[3] The clause may also stipulate which rules are to be followed for the mediation.[4] Often the place of the mediation will be specified as well as the language in which the mediation is to be conducted.

Any disputes remaining unsettled after mediation are then to be arbitrated, although the records of the mediation are to remain confidential and not to be introduced during the arbitration. As with the mediation clause, the arbitration clause will designate how the arbitrator is to be appointed and the rules the arbitration must follow,[5] along with the applicable location and language.

Some of these combined mediation and arbitration provisions fail to put a time limit on how long the mediation efforts may take, thereby allowing one of the parties, more likely the one at fault or facing a required payment, to frustrate the whole process.

Because the results of the arbitration are likely to be final and binding on the parties, with recourse to the courts thereafter only in very limited circumstances, the arbitration clause may provide more particular guidance to the parties than the mediation clause. The arbitration clause will generally outline the scope of the arbitration, identifying which issues may be arbitrated and which issues may not. However, the exclusion of certain issues can result in multiple proceedings.

In providing for the selection of impartial and neutral arbitrators, the arbitration clause will specify how many arbitrators are to be selected, and what skills or qualifications the arbitrators should possess. For a smaller company with a relatively low valuation, the arbitration clause in its unanimous shareholder agreement will probably require just one arbitrator. As three arbitrators definitely cost more, and involve more complicated proceedings, their involvement is more appropriate when the issues are quiet complex and a significant amount of money is at stake. Yet under many sets of arbitration rules, three arbitrators is the default structure in the absence of the parties agreeing that only one arbitrator will be necessary. Ordinarily the costs of arbitration will be shared equally by the parties involved.

Some arbitration clauses will set out certain special rules which are intended to override the set of general rules otherwise selected. For example, the clause may address how and when documents are to be exchanged, when hearings are to take place, and the deadline for rendering any decision, all of which are otherwise normally determined in the discretion of the arbitrator under the general rules.

More importantly, some clauses restrict or expand upon the relief that the arbitrator may award under the general rules. They may address whether the arbitrator can or cannot award interim or permanent injunctions, or order a party to perform the agreement, or award monetary damages.

While most arbitration decisions are final, the arbitration clause may grant specific rights to appeal, whether to a court or to a second arbitration panel. It may also specify how a decision is to be enforced. The parties are often permitted to enter a decision with the courts in each jurisdiction where enforcement may be needed.

DERIVATIVE ACTION

A shareholder may generally take over a company lawsuit the company is not prosecuting or defend a lawsuit the company is not defending. With the permission or leave of the court, the shareholder may bring what is called a "derivative action" in the name and on behalf of the company or one of its subsidiaries to enforce a right of the company, or to intervene in an action to which the company or a subsidiary is a party, for the purpose of prosecuting, defending or discontinuing the action on behalf of the company or subsidiary.[6]

The need for leave of the court is to prevent frivolous or vexatious actions. The court has to be satisfied before granting leave that the shareholder has given the company directors at least 14 days notice of her intention to apply to the court, that she is acting in good faith, and that the action itself is in the interest of the company to be prosecuted, defended or discontinued. Obtaining leave is not easy, given that the shareholder may not be aware of all the relevant facts, and that the directors have already weighed the costs and benefits of the proposed action and decided not to pursue it.

In addition to authorizing the shareholder or some other party to control the conduct of the action, the court may order that any amount adjudged payable by a defendant in the action shall be paid directly to the company's current or former shareholders and not to the company, and may order that the company pay the legal expenses of the shareholder incurred in connection with the action.[7]

OPPRESSION REMEDY

The CBCA provides that a court may make an order to rectify the results of certain "oppressive" conduct. The conduct may be a specific act or omission of the company, or the manner in which the company has carried on business, or the manner in which the directors have exercised their powers. Conduct that is not oppressive but is still unfairly prejudicial or that unfairly disregards the interests of any security holder, creditor, director, or officer can give rise to a remedy. Rectification can also be ordered in respect of similar conduct involving the company's affiliates.[8]

The court is empowered to make any order it thinks fit. It may order, for example, the appointment of a receiver, the amendment of the company's articles, by-laws or unanimous shareholder agreement, the issue, exchange or purchase of securities, or the appointment or replacement of directors. It may also order the setting aside of a company transaction, provide for the compensation of aggrieved persons, or even require the liquidation and dissolution of the company.[9]

In examining the conduct complained of, the court generally first assesses whether the conduct breached the complainant's reasonable expectations, and then goes on to determine whether the conduct amounted to oppression, unfair prejudice or unfair disregard. Because an oppression action is regarded as an "equitable" remedy, the court looks at business realities, not simply narrow legalities, and attempts to enforce not what is just legal but also what is fair.

In deciding if a complainant's expectations are reasonable in the first place, a court will generally look at the facts of the particular case, the relationships involved, and the entire context in which the challenged conduct occurs, including the existence of any conflicting claims and expectations. Fair treatment is essentially what shareholders are entitled to reasonably expect.

There are a number of specific factors a court may find useful in assessing the reasonableness of a complainant's expectations.[10]

Commercial practice is an important influence in the formation of a shareholder's expectations, and any departure from such practice that frustrates the exercise of the complainant's rights represents a significant factor to be considered by the court when deciding whether a remedy should be given.

The nature, size and structure of the company represent additional factors that are relevant in assessing the reasonableness of a complainant's expectations. The court may give more leeway to the directors of a small, closely-held company than to the directors of a larger, more widely-held company.

Reasonable expectations may also be influenced by the extent of any personal relationships between the complainant and others within the company. The court may apply a different standard if the expectations reflect relationships based on family or friendship ties rather than being between arm's length shareholders.

Past practice is another factor the court may use in deciding whether a complainant's expectations were reasonable, especially if such practice relates to the participation of the complainant in the company's profits and governance. However, the court will recognize that past practice may have to be changed for commercial reasons and that expectations should be altered accordingly.

The court may also look at whether the complainant was in a position to have taken steps to protect herself from the prejudice she claims to have suffered and whether she was influenced by any representations made in any correspondence or offering material when she became a shareholder. A shareholder agreement may also be viewed as forming the basis for reasonable expectations.

Once the court has determined that the complainant's expectations were reasonable, it then attempts to decide if the expectations were breached by conduct amounting to oppression, unfair prejudice or unfair disregard. While oppression is often taken to mean harsh and abusive conduct, unfair prejudice is often seen as less offensive. Examples might include squeezing out a minority shareholder, paying dividends without a formal declaration, failing to disclose related party transactions, paying directors' fees that are higher than the industry norm, or preferring some shareholders with management fees.[11]

Unfair disregard is seen as even less offensive. Improperly reducing a shareholder dividend or failing to deliver property belonging to the complainant are examples of unfair disregard.[12]

Once it decides that the complainant's reasonable expectations were breached by one of these three categories of wrongful conduct, the court may then fashion any remedy it think fits to properly rectify what took place.

Family Businesses

As mentioned above, family businesses may generate their own special shareholder expectations. Many private companies are established to hold family investments, serve as vehicles for estate freezes, or operate family businesses in which various family members actively participate. The oppression remedy provided by the CBCA has resulted in a growing number of cases involving family disputes arising out of these private companies.

While family tax planning may have been the primary reason for a private company to have been established, the ongoing power of the company's founder in maintaining the structure often creates tension and disharmony as the other family members wish to become more involved.

For example, under an estate freeze, the founder may wish to transfer the benefits of future growth of her company to her children in order to minimize taxes. While initially treating all of her children equally with the company issuing to all of them the same number of common or "growth" shares, she may later change her mind and wish for just one of them to carry on with the company as her successor. However, in having created a structure with all siblings being treated equally, any children no longer receiving equal treatment may look to the possibility of commencing an oppression action to regain what they may have lost.

The prevalence of family businesses in the oppression cases involving private companies has influenced how estate freezes are now structured. In order to provide some flexibility to the freeze structure and allow the founder to change her mind or favour one child over another, the common or growth shares are issued instead to a family trust rather than to specific children directly. The trust can then empower the trustees to choose which children, as beneficiaries, should acquire the common shares from the trust when the appropriate time comes, which could be when the founder finally makes up her mind who is to succeed her as owner. The founder may not control the trust and is often just one of three trustees.

OTHER COURT APPLICATIONS

Appointment of Auditor

If a private company does not have an auditor, a shareholder may apply to the court for an order appointing and fixing the remuneration of an auditor for the company to hold office until an auditor is appointed by the shareholders. Such an order, however, may not be made if the shareholders have already resolved to dispense with an auditor, as described in the *Collective Statutory Shareholder Rights* chapter.[13]

Calling of Meeting

If it is impracticable to call or conduct a shareholder meeting in the manner prescribed in the company's by-laws or articles or under the CBCA, a shareholder entitled to vote at a meeting may ask the court to order that a meeting be called and conducted in such manner as the court deems fit.[14]

Compliance with CBCA

If the company or any of its directors, officers, employees, agents or auditors fails to comply with any requirement of the CBCA or the company's articles, by-laws or unanimous shareholder agreement, a shareholder may apply to the court for an order directing such person to comply or restraining any further non-compliance.[15]

Fix Fair Value of Shares

If the company fails to apply to a court to fix the fair value of a dissenting shareholder's shares when required to do so, the shareholder may apply to a court for the same purpose.[16]

Investigation of Company

A shareholder may apply to the court for an order directing that an investigation be made of the company and any of its affiliates. The investigation may be ordered if the business of the company or its affiliates has been carried on with intent to defraud any person, or has been oppressive or unfairly prejudicial, or has unfairly disregarded the interests of a shareholder. It may also be ordered if the company or any of its affiliates has been formed for a fraudulent or unlawful purpose or is being dissolved for such a purpose, or if persons connected with it have acted fraudulently or dishonestly.

The court's order may involve the appointment of an inspector to enter any premises, examine documents and records, carry out investigations, conduct hearings under oath, and eventually report to the court.[17]

Liquidation and Dissolution of Company

A shareholder may apply to the court to supervise the liquidation and dissolution of the company, or apply for an order that the company be dissolved, or liquidated and dissolved under the supervision of the court.[18] Dissolution may be ordered if the company has failed for two or more consecutive years to hold an annual meeting, or has denied the shareholder access to examine certain corporate records, or has failed to provide the shareholder with the required financial statements.

Dissolution may also be ordered if the court is satisfied that a unanimous shareholder agreement entitles the shareholder to demand dissolution after the occurrence of a specified event, or that it would be "just and equitable" for the company to be dissolved.[19] Dissolution may be just and equitable if, in the absence of a shareholder agreement with at least some form of dispute resolution mechanism, a company with just two shareholders is deadlocked and cannot function properly because of an irresolvable shareholder dispute.

Rectification of Records

If a shareholder believes that her name has been wrongly entered in the company's share register or other record, or her name has been deleted or omitted, she may apply to the court for an order to have the register or record rectified. In addition to rectification, the court may order that a meeting or dividend payment not occur before the rectification, and even order that the shareholder be compensated for any loss.[20]

Removal of Auditor

A shareholder may apply to the court for an order declaring an auditor to be disqualified from serving and the office of auditor to be vacant.[21] A person is disqualified from serving as an auditor if she fails to be independent of the company, its affiliates, or their directors and officers. An auditor fails to be independent if, among other things, she or her business partner is a director, officer or shareholder of the company or an affiliate.

Restrain Holding of Meeting

Where a shareholder's proposal for any annual meeting has been refused by the company, the shareholder may apply to the court for an order to restrain the holding of the meeting at which the proposal was to be presented and to make any other order it thinks fit.[22]

Set Aside Contract

If any director or officer of the company fails to disclose her interest in any material contract with the company, a shareholder may apply to the court to have the contract set aside, or to require the director or officer to account to the company for any profit made on the contract.[23]

Settle Controversy over Elections

A shareholder may apply to the court to determine any controversy over the election or appointment of any director or auditor of the company. The court may make any order it thinks fit, including an order restraining a director or auditor from acting pending the determination of the dispute or declaring the result of a disputed election or appointment.

It may also order a new election or appointment, and provide directions for the management of the company's business in the meantime, as well as determine the voting rights of shareholders and of persons claiming to be shareholders.[24]

Conclusion

Although the directors have the statutory power and duty to manage the company's business and affairs, the shareholders can become more knowledgeable about how the company is run should they choose to do so. The power of the directors is subject to the specific rights granted to the shareholders. After all, ultimate control of the company is supposed to lie with the shareholders who elect the directors.

Yet the shareholders are usually neither informed nor consulted by the directors after the election until the next annual meeting.

This book has attempted to make the shareholders aware of the various means available to them to become more involved in the company. It has attempted to explain how they might change things they feel need to be changed. It has attempted to describe what they can do other than simply wait around for the next annual meeting.

While they possess numerous individual and collective rights under the CBCA, and likely many additional rights under the terms of their shares or in the company's articles and by-laws, some of the most significant rights they enjoy may well come to them by way of contract. These contractual rights are often set out in a unanimous shareholder agreement, and sometimes in a subscription agreement.

However, even though the shareholders may be aware of their various rights, they may choose not to exercise them. They may simply not see any need to become more active as shareholders. Or when they do see a need, they may then feel that they're too late to do much about it. Or that it's not worth fighting for. Despite the many alternative actions described in the previous chapter, none may appear to be very attractive to a shareholder. The costs, delays and uncertainty associated with court applications may be a sufficient deterrent from pursing most of them.

Perhaps except for one. Getting out, or getting the other shareholders out, may be the only acceptable remedy to a shareholder who can't get along with the others.

In the absence of a public market for the company's shares, and in the absence of any buy-sell provisions in a unanimous shareholder agreement or separate buy-sell agreement, the shareholder may have to resort to the courts to achieve an exit from his investment. Even though the company may have a shareholder agreement, it may only allow shareholders to sell out to a third party if they have first offered their shares to the other shareholders and been turned down, and may say nothing about selling to the others in the absence of a third party offer.

If the company has just a few shareholders and is unable to properly function because they or their nominee directors are deadlocked and can't agree on anything, the shareholder may try to ask the court to wind up the company on the grounds that it would be "just and equitable" to do so. This is part of the liquidation and dissolution remedy described in the previous chapter. Alternatively, the shareholder may ask the court to order the others to buy his shares, or to sell their own shares to him, on the basis of the oppression remedy, also described in the previous chapter.

But by going to court in search of a way out, whether alleging that he has been oppressed by the company and the other shareholders, or asserting that the company is really a deadlocked partnership deserving of being wound up, he runs the risk that the court may prescribe a result he doesn't really want. If the court finds that he hasn't been treated all that badly by the others, he may end up worse off.

Although many cases have been reported involving these types of claims, looking at just a few may be useful reminders of what can happen when going the litigation route. The following four cases all involved companies with only a few shareholders, whose conduct towards each other was held not to be oppressive, and whose relationships were not subject to any buy-sell agreements. The shareholders concerned did nothing wrong and weren't at fault, but nonetheless found themselves without a clear way to change their circumstances.

One case[1] involved two brothers who owned 20 per cent of a cookie business. They were engaged in "a finger-pointing poisonous stand-off" with a husband and wife who owned the remaining 80 per cent. Both sides wanted out but had no mechanism for selling their shares. The court imposed one, by ordering that they establish a two button buzzer system that would identify the first side to push its button while the share price would be dropping every six seconds from a specified starting value. The side that did not fix the price would have the option of requiring the other to buy or sell at the fixed price, although the party required to buy could decline by selling at a 20 per cent discount. On appeal, this buzzer system was rejected, and the appeal court ordered the company to buy out the brothers' 20 per cent interest at a value to be determined by an independent valuator.

Yet the parties each experienced the feeling of having an unexpected solution imposed upon them.

Another case[2] concerned four brothers who each owned 25 per cent of a disposal services business. When the son of one them established a competing business, causing the "once harmonious relationship" among the brothers to be "irreparably broken down", the brother with the ambitious son asked the court to order the others to buy him out. The court refused, holding that their 20 year old shareholder agreement would not be amended to include a buy-sell provision.

A further case[3] featured a father and son who jointly owned two-thirds of a pharmacy business, with another pharmacist owning the remaining third. While the father and son wanted to buy out the pharmacist, and the pharmacist wanted to buy out the father and son, neither side could agree on how to proceed. The pharmacist ended up asking the court to order that the entire business be sold by public auction. The court responded by ordering that his shares be purchased by the father and son at fair value.

And the last case[4] dealt with a husband and wife going through divorce proceedings who lacked a mechanism for allowing one of them to sell out of the professional conference business which they owned 50-50. In finding that the wife "justifiably lost confidence" in her husband as a business partner, the court ordered a transfer of the husband's shares to the wife at fair market value.

Had the parties in these four cases entered into buy-sell agreements with each other before they realized they wanted to get out, they may have been able to go their separate ways a lot faster. And maybe a lot more cheaply, depending on their legal fees and the court's award of costs. Because buy-sell agreements prescribe an exit mechanism that was lacking in the foregoing cases, the certainty they provide may be preferable to the uncertainty of going to court in search of a resolution.

While these cases illustrate to a shareholder the specific advantages of buy-sell provisions in a unanimous shareholder agreement or separate buy-sell agreement, they also illustrate the broader advantages of having his special expectations as a shareholder reduced to contractual form. Any benefits he expects to receive as a shareholder that do not flow directly from the individual or collective statutory rights described earlier in this book should be set out in an agreement with the company and the other shareholders as a way of avoiding some of the unexpected results reflected in these cases. The courts prefer to enforce contracts, not ignore them or re-write them, so long as the contracts have unambiguous terms.

But having contractual protection hardly guarantees a shareholder a predictable, let alone harmonious, experience as a private company shareholder. While comprehensive agreements may provide some comfort, they are still contracts that may prove their worth only as a last resort, when negotiation and moral suasion fail to achieve compliance and recourse to the courts in a lawsuit for damages or specific performance may be the only alternative.

Despite the advantages of having enforceable contracts, a shareholder may be as well or better served though the implementation of some of the recommended practices described in the *Governance* chapter. With proper governance structures and procedures in place, at least some of the behaviour within the company which might otherwise give rise to a breach of contract claim before a court might be avoided altogether.

Good governance might also help to reduce the possibility of a shareholder's rights and expectations being frustrated or ignored in the absence of any agreement with the shareholder. At least it may detect and deter the kinds of behaviour that can lead to claims of shareholder oppression.

For example, the failure to simulate arm's-length transactions when dealing with related parties, the lack of good faith on the part of the directors, or the benefiting of majority shareholders to the exclusion of minority shareholders, are more likely to be avoided when the company has a board and audit committee with independent directors and has a code of business conduct which addresses conflicts of interest.

As described earlier, it is often difficult to fully implement good governance in the private company context. But whichever governance structures and procedures the company decides to implement, it will nonetheless be influenced by what other private companies with which it competes, perhaps ones it envies, are also doing at the same time.

Despite the cynical view some managers may have that the recommended structures and procedures are mere window-dressing, good governance may become commonplace. It may become an indicator of the well-managed private company. It won't be looked at as a quick-fix management technique that falls in and out of fashion. It will instead be looked at as having enduring value, respected for no better reason than it's just the way things are done.

For those who remain as shareholders of a private company, they should encourage good governance as well as good contracts as the way to avoid shareholder disputes, so that the motivations and expectations they had when they first became shareholders may continue to be met.

Endnotes

Introduction

1. R.S.C. 1985, c. C-44.
2. Section 2(1) of the CBCA Regulations defines a "distributing corporation" as a "reporting issuer" under certain provincial securities legislation, or if not a "reporting issuer", a corporation which has filed a prospectus or registration statement, or which has securities listed on a stock exchange, or which has amalgamated or been reorganized with a corporation which has done so.
3. See the definition of "private issuer" in section 2.4(1) of National Instrument 45-106 *Prospectus and Registration Exemption*. The number of shareholders is limited to 50, excluding employees and former employees.
4. Section 263 of the CBCA and section 5 of the CBCA Regulations.
5. Subsection 21(3) of the CBCA.
6. Subsection 50(4) of the CBCA provides that the registration of the issue of shares in the register is complete and valid registration for all purposes Subsection 51(1) of the CBCA provides that the company may treat the registered shareholder as the person exclusively entitled to vote, to receive notices, to receive any interest, dividend or other payments in respect of the shares, and otherwise to exercise all the rights and powers of an owner of the shares.
7. Subsection 25(1) of the CBCA.
8. Subsection 25(3) of the CBCA.
9. Subsection 45(1) of the CBCA provides shareholder immunity from the liabilities, acts and defaults of the company except for liability under subsections 38(4) [improper return of capital], 118(4) and (5) [improper distributions], 146(5) [directors' liabilities assumed under a unanimous shareholder agreement], and 226(4) and (5) [distributions made upon the company's dissolution if claims are made within two years following the dissolution].

The case law also provides certain exceptions from such immunity, as occurs when a shareholder (often the only shareholder) is the company's *alter ego* and the company is almost a sham used to perpetrate dishonest actions, or acts merely as the shareholder's agent.

Chapter 2 – Individual Statutory Rights

1 Subsection 24(3) of the CBCA.
2 Section 27 of the CBCA.
3 Subsection 24(4) of the CBCA.
4 Subsection 21(1) of the CBCA.
5 Subsection 20(1) of the CBCA.
6 Subsection 120(6 1) of the CBCA.
7 Subsection 21(1) of the CBCA.
8 Subsection 21(2) of the CBCA.
9 Subsection 138(4) of the CBCA.
10 Subsection 21(3) of the CBCA.
11 Subsection 21(7) of the CBCA.
12 Subsection 21(6) of the CBCA.
13 Section 190 of the CBCA.
14 Subsection 157(2) of the CBCA.
15 Subsection 159(1) of the CBCA.
16 Part 8 of the CBCA Regulations.
17 Paragraph 24(3)(b) of the CBCA.
18 Section 42 of the CBCA.
19 Subsection 43(1) of the CBCA.
20 Paragraph 24(3)(c) of the CBCA.
21 Subsection 226(4) of the CBCA.
22 Section 49 of the CBCA.
23 Section 80 of the CBCA.
24 Subsection 168(2) of the CBCA.
25 Section 143 of the CBCA.
26 Section 150 of the CBCA and sections 60 to 64 of the CBCA Regulations.
27 Section 137 of the CBCA and Part 6 of the CBCA Regulations.
28 Subsection 149(2) of the CBCA.
29 Section 175 of the CBCA.
30 Section 140 of the CBCA.
31 Section 148 of the CBCA.

32 Section 141 of the CBCA.
33 Section 145.1 of the CBCA.

Chapter 3 – Collective Statutory Rights

1 Subsection 117(1) of the CBCA.
2 Subsection 2(1) of the CBCA.
3 Subsections 176(6) and 189(8) of the CBCA.
4 Section 183 of the CBCA.
5 Section 184 of the CBCA.
6 Section 181 of the CBCA.
7 Section 186 of the CBCA.
8 Subsection 182(1) of the CBCA.
9 See *Re Canada (Director appointed under section 260 of the Business Corporations Act*), (1991) 3 O.R.(3d) 336, 80 D.L.R. (4th) 619 (C.A.).
10 Subsections 176(1) and (5) of the CBCA.
11 Subsection 162(1) of the CBCA.
12 Section 163 of the CBCA.
13 Section 165 of the CBCA.
14 Subsection 103(2) of the CBCA.
15 Section 188 of the CBCA.
16 Subsection 106(3) of the CBCA.
17 Section 109 of the CBCA.
18 Sections 103 and 173 of the CBCA.
19 Any proceedings to dissolve or liquidate the company must be stayed if it is found to be insolvent under subsection 2(1) of the *Bankruptcy and Insolvency Act,* R.S.C. 1985, c. B-3.
20 Sections 210 and 211 of the CBCA.
21 Section 227 of the CBCA.
22 Section 194 of the CBCA.
23 Subsection 49(18) of the CBCA.
24 Subsections 26(1) to (3) of the CBCA.
25 Subsection 26(5) of the CBCA.
26 Section 38 of the CBCA.
27 Subsections 189(3) to (9) of the CBCA.
28 See *Benson v. Third Canadian General Investment Trust* (1993), 1993 CarswellOnt 166, 14 O.R. (3d) 493, 13 B.L.R. (2d) 265 (Ont. Gen. Div. [Commercial List]).

Chapter 4 – Additional Shareholder Rights

1 Section 28 of the CBCA.

2 See subsections 34(2) and 36(2) of the CBCA.

3 Section 107 of the CBCA.

Chapter 5 – Buy-Sell Rights

1 Subsection 84(3) of the *Income Tax Act* (Canada) (the "ITA") provides that a share repurchase by a corporation entails a deemed dividend to the seller of the shares for the amount paid in excess of the paid up capital on those shares. Because the amount is treated as a dividend and not as a capital gain, the amount cannot be included in the taxpayer's lifetime capital gains exemption. Section 54 of the ITA in defining "proceeds of disposition" excludes in subparagraph (j) "any amount that would otherwise be proceeds of disposition of a share to the extent that the amount is deemed by subsection 84(2) or (3) to be a dividend received and is not deemed by paragraph 55(2)(a) or subparagraph 88(2)(b)(ii) not to be a dividend".

Chapter 6 – Unanimous Shareholder Agreements

1 Subsection 146(10) of the CBCA.

2 See for example *Motherwell v. Schoof*, 1949 CarswellAlta 50, [1949] 2 W.W.R. 529, [1949] 4 D.L.R. 812 (Alta. T.D.) and *Ringuet v. Bergeron*, 1960 CarswellQue 46, [1960] S.C.R. 672, 24 D.L.R. (2d) 449 (S.C.C.).

3 Subsection 102(1) of the CBCA.

4 See *Duha Printers (Western) Ltd. v. R.*, [1998] 1 S.C.R. 795, 1998 CarswellNat 750, 1998 CarswellNat 751 (S.C.C.).

5 Subsection 146(1) of the CBCA.

6 Subsection 6(3) of the CBCA.

7 Paragraph 49(8)(c) of the CBCA.

8 Subsection 146(2) of the CBCA.

9 Subsection 146(5) of the CBCA.

10 Section 119 of the CBCA.

11 Paragraph 122(1)(a) of the CBCA.

12 See *Elsley v. J.G. Collins Insurance Agencies Ltd.*, [1978] 2 S.C.R. 916, *H.L. Staebler Company Ltd. v. Allan* (2008), 92 O.R. (3d) 107 (C.A.), and *Shafron v. KRG Insurance Brokers (Western) Inc.*, 2009 SCC 6.

Chapter 7 – Shareholder Meetings

1 Section 142 of the CBCA.
2 Subsection 144(2) of the CBCA.
3 Subsection 133(1) of the CBCA, although the company may apply to the court for an order extending the time for calling an annual meeting.
4 Section 155 of the CBCA.
5 Section 162 of the CBCA.
6 Section 106 of the CBCA.
7 Section 103 of the CBCA.
8 Subsection 135(5) of the CBCA.
9 Section 132 of the CBCA.
10 Subsections 132(4) and (5) and 141(3) and (4) of the CBCA, and section 45 of the CBCA Regulations. A shareholder entitled to vote may vote by means of a telephonic, electronic or other communication facility if the facility enables the votes to be gathered in a manner that permits their subsequent verification and permits the tallied votes to be presented to the company without it being possible for the company to identify how each shareholder or group of shareholders voted.
11 Part 5 of the CBCA Regulations.
12 Subsection 135(1.1) of the CBCA.
13 Subsection 135(2) of the CBCA.
14 Subsection 135(6) of the CBCA.
15 See *Anderson Lumber Co. v. Canadian Conifer Ltd.* 1977 CarswellAlta 159, [1977] 5 W.W.R. 41, 77 D.L.R. (3d) 126, 25 C.B.R. (N.S.) 35, 4 A.R. 282 (Alta C.A.).
16 Subsections 135(3) and (4).
17 Subsection 139(1) of the CBCA.
18 Subsections 139(2) and (3) of the CBCA.

Chapter 8 – Director Duties

1 Subsection 115(1) of the CBCA.
2 Subsection 189(2) of the CBCA.
3 Subsection 115(3) of the CBCA.
4 Section 171 of the CBCA.
5 Paragraph 122(1)(a) of the CBCA.

6 See *BCE Inc. v. 1976 Debentureholders*, 2008 SCC 69, at paragraphs 37 and 38.

7 See *People's Department Stores Ltd. (1992) Inc., Re*, 2004 CarswellQue 2862, 2004 CarswellQue 2863, [2004] S.C.J. No. 64, REJB 2004-72160, (*sub nom.* Peoples Department Stores Inc. (Bankrupt) v. Wise) 326 N.R. 267 (Eng.), (*sub nom.* Peoples Department Stores Inc. (Bankrupt) v. Wise) 326 N.R. 267 (Fr.), 4 C.B.R. (5th) 215, [2004] 3 S.C.R. 461, 2004 SCC 68, (*sub nom.* Peoples Department Stores Inc. (Trustee of) v. Wise) 244 D.L.R. (4th) 564, 49 B.L.R. (3d) 165 (S.C.C.).

8 Subsection 120(1) of the CBCA.

9 Subsection 120(2) of the CBCA.

10 Subsection 120(4) of the CBCA.

11 Subsection 120(5) of the CBCA.

12 Subsection 120(7) of the CBCA.

13 Subsection 120(7.1) of the CBCA.

14 See *Canadian Aero Service Ltd. v. O'Malley* [1974] S.C.R. 592 (S.C.C.), and *International Corona Resources Ltd. v. LAC Minerals Ltd.* , [1989] S.C.J. No. 83, EYB 1989-67469, 1989 CarswellOnt 126, 1989 CarswellOnt 965, 44 B.L.R. 1, 35 E.T.R. 1, (*sub nom.* LAC Minerals Ltd. v. International Corona Resources Ltd.) 69 O.R. (2d) 287, (*sub nom.* LAC Minerals Ltd. v. International Corona Resources Ltd.) 61 D.L.R. (4th) 14, 101 N.R. 239, 36 O.A.C. 57, [1989] 2 S.C.R. 574, 6 R.P.R. (2d) 1, 26 C.P.R. (3d) 97 (S.C.C.).

15 Paragraph 122(1)(b) of the CBCA.

16 Subsection 123(4) of the CBCA.

17 See the *Peoples* decision in note 7.

18 See the *Peoples* decision in note 7, and *Maple Leaf Foods Inc. v. Schneider Corp.* (1998) 42 O.R. (3d) 177 (Ont. C.A.).

19 See *UPM-Kymmene Corp. v. UPM-Kymmene Miramichi Inc.*, (2002), 2002 CarswellOnt 2096, [2002] O.J. No. 2412, 19 C.C.E.L. (3d) 203, 27 B.L.R. (3d) 53, 214 D.L.R. (4th) 496, 32 C.C.P.B. 120 (Ont. S.C.J. [Commercial List])

20 Subsections 34(2), 35(3) and 36(2) and paragraph 115(3)(e) of the CBCA.

21 Paragraph 118(2)(a) of the CBCA.

22 Subsection 118(4) of the CBCA.

23 Sections 30 to 33 and subsection 39(6) of the CBCA.

24 Subsection 159(1) of the CBCA.

25 Section 121 of the CBCA.

26 Section 122 of the CBCA.

27 Section 41 of the CBCA.

28 Paragraph 118(2)(b) of the CBCA.
29 Subsection 189(1) of the CBCA.
30 Subsections 122(2) and (3) of the CBCA.
31 Section 42 and paragraph 115(3)(d) of the CBCA.
32 Paragraph 118(2)(c) of the CBCA.
33 Subsection 118(4) of the CBCA.
34 Subsection 123(4) of the CBCA.
35 See *McClurg v. Canada* [1990] 1990 CarswellNat 520, 1990 CarswellNat 743, 3 S.C.R. 1020 (S.C.C.) and *Neuman v. Minister of National Revenue*, [1998] 1998 CarswellNat 685, 1998 CarswellNat 686, 1 S.C.R. 770 (S.C.C.)
36 Section 43 of the CBCA.
37 Paragraph 115(3)(b) of the CBCA.
38 Section 125 of the CBCA.
39 Paragraph 115(3)(c) and subsections 25(3) and (4) of the CBCA.
40 Subsection 118(1) of the CBCA.
41 Section 103 of the CBCA.
42 Subsection 124(1) of the CBCA.
43 Subsection 124(2) of the CBCA.
44 Subsections 124(3) and (5) of the CBCA.
45 See *Blair v. Consolidated Enfield Corp.*, 1995 CarswellOnt 1393, EYB 1995-67681, 1995 CarswellOnt 1179, 128 D.L.R. (4th) 73, 187 N.R. 241, 86 O.A.C. 245, 25 O.R. (3d) 480 (note), 24 B.L.R. (2d) 161, [1995] 4 S.C.R. 5 (S.C.C.).
46 See *Bennett v. Bennett Environmental Inc.*, 2009 CarswellOnt 1132, 2009 ONCA 198 (Ont. C.A.).
47 Subsection 124(6) of the CBCA.

Chapter 9 – Governance

1 See National Policy 58-201 *Corporate Governance Guidelines*, National Instrument 58-101 *Disclosure of Corporate Governance Practices*, and National Instrument 52-110 *Audit Committees*. As of the time of writing, the Canadian Securities Administrators have proposed a repeal of the governance "best practices" set out in the foregoing policy, to be replaced by nine principles of governance. Of the nine proposed principles, three represent new items that are not specifically addressed in the current policy. One item deals with the need to establish a system of oversight and management of actual and potential conflicts of interest. Another item deals with the need for a framework of risk oversight and management. The third item deals with the

need for the board to stay informed of shareholder views through the shareholder meeting process as well as through ongoing dialogue.

2 Public companies that are "venture issuers" as defined in National Instrument 58-101 are partially relieved from providing the governance disclosure required of larger listed companies.

Chapter 10 – Dispute Resolution and Remedies

1 Subsection 122(1) of the CBCA.

2 *BCE Inc. v. 1976 Debentureholders*, 2008 SCC 69.

3 For example, the ADR Institute of Ontario.

4 For example, the National Mediation Rules of the ADR Institute of Canada, Inc.

5 For example, the National Arbitration Rules of the ADR Institute of Canada, Inc., or for shorter timelines and expedited procedures, the Simplified Arbitration Rules of the ADR Institute of Canada, Inc.

6 Section 239 of the CBCA.

7 Section 240 of the CBCA.

8 Section 241 of the CBCA.

9 See *The Canadian Oppression Remedy Judicially Considered: 1995-2001* (2004) 30 Queen's L.J., a survey of the oppression remedy conducted by Professors Ben-Ishai and Puri which includes the results of a second study for the period December 2001 to February 2004. Of the 71 cases considered in their first study, 92 per cent dealt with private, closely-held companies. The authors observed, at page 89, that the majority of the successful oppression actions in the period of the first study involved the diversion of corporate profits, personal use of corporate profits by those controlling the corporation, the exclusion of the applicant from the operations of the corporation, or the alteration of proportional shareholdings. The remedy most often granted was a share purchase, usually in the context of a closely-held corporation where the shareholders lost confidence in each other and could not continue to work together.

10 Paragraphs 73 to 80 of the *BCE Inc.* decision described in note 2.

11 Paragraph 93 of the *BCE Inc.* decision described in note 2.

12 Paragraph 94 of the *BCE Inc.* decision described in note 2.

13 Section 167 of the CBCA.

14 Subsection 144(1) of the CBCA.

15 Section 247 of the CBCA.

16 Subsection 190(16) of the CBCA.
17 Part XIX of the CBCA.
18 Subsections 211(8) and 213(3) of the CBCA.
19 Subsection 214(1) of the CBCA.
20 Section 243 of the CBCA.
21 Subsection 161(4) of the CBCA.
22 Subsection 137(8) of the CBCA.
23 Subsection 120(8) of the CBCA.
24 Section 145 of the CBCA.

Chapter 11 – Conclusion

1 See *Re Wittlin et al. and Bergman et al* (1996), 25 O.R (3d) 761 (C.A.), reversing (1994), 19 O.R. (3d) 145 (Gen. Div.).
2 See *Re Lecce et al v. Lecce et al* (1990), 72 O.R. (2d) 540 (H.C.).
3 See *Re Footitt et al v. Gleason et al* (1996), 25 O.R (3d) 729 (Gen. Div.).
4 See *Re Bellman v. Bellman et al* (1996), 26 O.R. (3d) 56 (Gen. Div.).

Index

DIRECTOR DUTIES
- acquisition of shares, 79
- appointment of officers, 80
- borrowing, 80
- by-laws, passing, 83
- commissions, authorizing payment of, 80
- compliance with
  - *Canada Business Corporations Act*, 80
  - company charter, 80
- dividends, declaration of, 81
- duty of care
  - business judgment rule, 78
  - generally, 77
- fiduciary duty
  - conflicts of interest, disclosure of, 76
  - corporate opportunity, avoiding misuse, 77
  - generally, 75
- financial statements, approval of, 79
- generally, 73
- indemnification, 83
- insurance, 83
- issuance of shares, 82
- officers, appointment of, 80
- passing by-laws, 83
- payment of commissions, authorizing, 80
- redemption of shares, 79
- remuneration, fixing, 82
- shares, issuance of, 82
- vacancies
  - auditor, 82
  - director, 82

DISPUTE RESOLUTION AND REMEDIES
- arbitration, 94
- court applications
  - auditor
    - appointment, 100
    - removal, 101
  - elections, settle controversy over, 102
  - compliance with *Canada Business Corporations Act*, 100
  - contract, set aside, 102
  - dissolution of company, 101, 104
  - fix fair value of shares, 100
  - investigation of company, 100
  - liquidation of company, 101, 104
  - meetings,
    - calling of, 100
    - restrain holding of, 102
  - rectification of records, 101
- derivative action, 96
- generally, 93
- mediation, 94
- oppression remedy
  - family businesses, 99
  - generally, 97, 104

GOVERNANCE
- benefits, 86
- generally, 85, 106

implementation, 87, 91
recommended structures and practices
audit committee, 89
board and independent directors, 89
board assessments, 91
code of business conduct and ethics, 90
compensation committee, 90
continuing education, 91
director orientation, 91
generally, 88
nominating committee, 90
resistance to, 86

PRIVATE COMPANY
definition, 3

REMEDIES, *see* DISPUTE RESOLUTION AND REMEDIES

SHAREHOLDER, *see also* SHAREHOLDER MEETINGS; SHAREHOLDER RIGHTS; UNANIMOUS SHAREHOLDER AGREEMENTS
definition, 4
expectations, 4

SHAREHOLDER AGREEMENTS, see UNANIMOUS SHAREHOLDER AGREEMENTS

SHAREHOLDER MEETINGS
adjournment of, 69
annual meetings, 68
conduct of, 70
generally, 67
notice of, 69
place of, 68
preparation for, 70
special meetings, 68

SHAREHOLDER RIGHTS
buy-sell rights
auction rights, 49
drag-along rights, 45
first refusal rights, 42
generally, 41, 104
piggyback rights, 44
shotgun rights, 48
transfer rights, 46
valuation of transferred shares, 47
collective statutory rights
amalgamation, 18
amending articles, 20
auditors
right to appoint, 21
right to remove, 21
by-laws, 21
continuance, 23
directors
right to elect, 24
right to remove, 24
right to restrict powers, 24
dissolution, 24
generally, 17
liquidation, 24
squeeze-out, 25
stated capital
right to increase, 26
right to reduce, 27
transfer of all assets, 27
conversion rights, 30
dilution protection rights, 31
dividend rights, 32
generally, 4, 30
individual statutory rights
appraisal, *see* dissent and appraisal
company dividends, *see* receipt of company dividends
company property, receipt of on dissolution, 11
corporate records
right to copies, 8
right to examine corporate records, 8
right to examine shareholder list, 9
right to receive shareholder list, 9
dissent and appraisal, 9
financial statement
right to examine, 10
right to receive, 10

generally, 7
receipt of company dividends, 10
share certificates
replacement, right to receive, 13
right to receive, 12
shareholder meetings
auditor attendance, right to require, 13
proposals, right to submit, 14
proxies, right to solicit, 14
requisition meeting, right to, 13
vote, right to, 15
information rights, 34
liquidation rights, 34
loss of rights, 40
nomination rights, 35
pre-emptive rights, 36
redemption rights, 36
registration rights, 38
veto rights, 39
voting rights, 39
withdrawal of rights, 40

UNANIMOUS SHAREHOLDER AGREEMENTS
amending procedure, 65
bank financing, 58
board representation, 54
covenants, *see* family law covenants; negative covenants
day-to-day operations, 65
family law covenants, 64
generally, 51
guarantees, 58
major decisions, 56
management representation, 54
mandatory shareholder funding, 59
miscellaneous matters, 65
negative covenants
enforcement, 63
generally, 60
non-competition covenant, 62
non-disclosure covenant, 61
non-solicitation covenant, 61
pre-emptive rights, 58
procedural matters, 65
profits, use of, 57
reasons for, 53
termination of, 65